RICHES FOR WITCHES
CREATING A MAGICAL LIFE OF ABUNDANCE
SHEENA CUNDY

*Dear Kate
It's time to be rich!
Blessings be yours...
Sheena ✪*

SHEENA CUNDY

Copyright © 2023 by Sheena Cundy

All rights reserved.

No portion of this book may be reproduced in any form without written permission from the publisher or author, except as permitted by U.S. copyright law.

Published by Treehouse Magic

SheenaCundy.com

Edited by Laura Perry

LauraPerryAuthor.com

Cover Design: fionajaydemedia.com

Formatting: atticus.io

Images: Deposit Photos

TABLE OF CONTENTS

Dedication	V
Epigraph	VI
What People are Saying	VII
Foreword	X
Introduction	XII
PART 1 - DREAMING GOLD - Building Foundations	1
1. Tuning In to Riches	2
2. Wealthy Witch	10
3. Natural Abundance	19
4. The Power of Loving Intentions	27
5. The Practical Dreamer	36
6. Calling In The Masters	53
7. Tarot for Success	65
8. Meeting Amergin	72
9. Prosper with the Moon	78
PART II - DIGGING FOR GOLD - Doing the work	96

10. Going Deeper	97
11. Dark Riches	110
12. Magical Bonds	121
13. Working with the Warrior	129
14. Prosper with the Sun	142
PART III - FINDING GOLD - Sustaining and Sharing Your Riches	158
15. Money Consciousness	159
16. The Lessons of Money	167
17. Witch at Work	174
18. Magical Marketing	185
19. Abundance Heart-Set	199
20. The Broken Heart	207
21. In Service	219
22. Sharing Your Gifts	227
23. Celebrating the Magical Life	236
Thank you	244
Audio Links	245
Further Reading and Resources	247
Acknowledgments	250
Also By Sheena Cundy	251
About the Author	252

For Leon and George... who make my life *richer*.

Whatever you do, or dream you can, begin it.
Boldness has genius and power and magic in it.
GOETHE

WHAT PEOPLE ARE SAYING

'In the entertaining and informative *Riches for Witches*, Sheena Cundy cleverly draws her readers in, broadening their views from solely financially focused to a more holistic perspective. Through her guidance, readers explore what hinders their path, what has shaped individual views, and what might foster change. The gods may laugh when men pray to them for wealth, but not when they pray for an understanding of what has led to imbalance and what might be done to concretely attain wholeness.'

Timothy Roderick, author of *Wicca: A Year and A Day, Dark Moon Mysteries*, and other books.

'I get so tired of all those "just think and get rich" or "just say affirmations for prosperity" books that make it sound effortless. Thankfully, this isn't one of those. Sheena Cundy understands that it takes effort - both mundane and magical - to achieve your goals. And she has a well-thought-out plan for doing just that. One chapter at a time, one activity at a time, this book can help you work your way out of self-sabotage and toward clarity. No, it's not easy, and Cundy is honest about that. But she's also honest about something more important:

It's worth doing. So let her help you do it. You'll be glad you did.'

Laura Perry, author of *Ariadne's Thread: Awakening the Wonders of the Ancient Minoans in Our Modern Lives* and *Labrys & Horns: An Introduction to Modern Minoan Paganism.*

'Riches are more than just money. Although I'm sure everyone wants sufficient cash to pay the bills, we can get a sense of plenty from all aspects of our lives. It can be a fulfilling job, creative achievement, love and friendship, or contentment with our environment. In *Riches for Witches*, Sheena Cundy offers a variety of magical techniques for attracting the things we want more of and banishing self-limiting ideas that hold us back. These include journalling, self-reflection, spells, mantras, guided visualisations, divination, and crafting. This book contains a wealth of knowledge, experience and inspiration for anyone seeking spiritual and material abundance.'

Lucya Starza, author of *Candle Magic, Poppets and Magical Dolls, Scrying,* and *Rounding the Wheel of the Year*, and the novel, *Erosion.*

'With precision and delight, Sheena Cundy has created a joyful exploration of abundance and prosperity for witches of any path. Supported by lovely chants and a deep knowledge of the principles of magic, *Riches for Witches* is a manifestation of true creation. An excellent read, one that so many of us need!'

Lisa McSherry, author of *Travel Magic, A Witch's Guide to Crafting Your Practice*, and *The Virtual Pagan 2.0*

'This book blends pragmatism with magic in the best possible way. Even if you aren't a witchcraft practitioner, it's worth reading this book just for the questions and challenges it poses because there's a lot to consider and learn from here. Sheena Cundy takes on the idea that you can't just do magic for money, and shows us how to rethink our relationship with finances and abundance.'

Nimue Brown, author of *Earth Spirit: Beyond Sustainability – Authentic Living at a Time of Climate Crisis* and other books on Druidry and Paganism.

'A magical, lyrical journey to change your life. Sheena taps into what abundance and prosperity really mean, not just monetary but the whole shebang of what life has to offer. This is a real magical workout to make things happen for you and includes exercises, meditations, and musical links. Take the plunge!'
Rachel Patterson – High Priestess, Speaker, Teacher, and Best-selling author of over twenty-five books on Witchcraft and Magic.

'There is no fluff here. In *Riches for Witches*, Sheena Cundy offers a succinct and utterly practical guide to manifesting wealth in every area of your life. She's a down-to-earth and personable author whose tone is warm, light-hearted and encouraging. Her own sense of the wealth in her life shines through these pages, as does her years of dedication to the witch way.

You could not possibly read this book and feel you'd been short-changed. It is absolutely packed with tools, practices and even links to specially-created audio tracks to guide your pathworkings. An invaluable resource and a worthy sequel to *The Witch Wavelength*.'
Daniel Allison, Best-selling author of *Scottish Myths and Legends*.

FOREWORD

When Sheena asked me to write the foreword to the book you hold in your hands, I was enormously pleased. Why? Because here is exactly what you need to begin thinking in a different way about yourself, the world you live in, and how to live abundantly in the flow of it all.

I've always believed that the trick to living securely and with purpose in this world begins inside us, in our own vision, heart, and spirit. It's so easy to become uncertain and to live in fear because, let's face it, our society doesn't promote security and vision with its emphasis on materialism and division. But we are still creatures of soul and magic, and in *Riches for Witches*, Sheena takes you by the hand and shows you the way to tap into that magic, undo the programming of our upbringing and society, and flourish and prosper in the ways I believe we are truly meant to.

You see, abundance and richness are something we live – a path of the heart. It's a particular way of seeing and interacting with the world around us. It's a path that empowers rather than disenfranchises us and lets us be free of fear even during times of hardship.

I entreat you to follow the guidance in *Riches for Witches* and reclaim the joy that is your right. You'll learn to strengthen your spirit, flex your imagination, and step into the flow of your own natural abundance. I promise you won't be disappointed because this way of living is heart-led and true.

Katherine Genet – author of *The Wilde Grove Series*
New Zealand, 13 July 2023
www.katherinegenet.online

INTRODUCTION

I Am Rich in Mind, Body, Spirit and Pocket

A re you ready to enrich your life on every level?
I think you are.
Can you handle the abundance and prosperity that is your magical inheritance?
I know you can.
Welcome to the second book in *The Witch Wavelength* series. You don't need to have read the first book to read this one, though doing so would be helpful. *Riches for Witches* works as a stand-alone and is full of witchy richness. Literally.
I have long been an avid reader and student of success and prosperity principles, both in the magical and earthly spheres. So it gives me great pleasure to share with you the things I have learned so far and continue to practise every day.
I have always wanted to write a book like this but didn't think I was qualified enough for it.

What Happened?

Ten years ago I started writing stories about a crazy menopausal Witch called Minerva (*The Madness and the Magic*). It was my remedy for a mid-life crisis of ridiculous extremes. I discovered that by making up someone else's story, I could re-write my own. It was a form of magic.

After writing Minerva's story, the urge to create didn't leave me. I continued practising creativity as magic, and that practice became the foundation of a life of abundance. I have become a Witch who writes and works her magic through the power of words. The written word, spoken word, and words which I sing out on stage and into the wind... through music, stories and books like this one.

My creative work fills me with a whole lot of love and joy. It's a magical life. Not always plain sailing, but with experience and the tools of my craft, I have learned to ride the waves.

Getting rich can be something that begs lots of questions, most of them moralistic in nature. I struggled with them for a long time and maybe you do too. Questions like:

- Shouldn't I get rich first and *then* tell people how to do it?
- Should a Witch even *want* to be rich? Is it allowed?
- Do I have to be a millionaire to prove this stuff works?

Yes, I know, it's not easy to read. And no, I haven't become a millionaire through practising abundance. But I have gone from feeling poor to feeling rich. From feeling unworthy to feeling worthy. And now that my days are consistently full of feeling this way, how could I not share that good fortune with you?

In *The Witch Wavelength* we worked with the elements as a means of tuning into our magical nature – the soul essence – to realise our dreams and visions. In *Riches for Witches*, we're talking about the vibration of **Abundance,** one of the highest energetic frequencies there is.

We are building upon what we have already created with the elements of Air, Fire, Water, Earth and Spirit, in the first book. We are going to travel further into the territory of vibrational frequency… very much on the witch wavelength with all the magic that's needed for the journey. Get ready to fly, Magical One.

Are you ready to up your game?

On a magical level, you will be combining your Air nature – your thoughts and your mindset – with your Fire nature to stoke the flames of your creative potential. That potential is the magic inside you waiting for direction. As soon as your Water nature receives it and begins to flow in every good way, the universe will get the message, and you will begin to manifest with the full power of your Earth nature.

Once you have grounded the elements within and can work with them as part of your own nature, you will have a solid formula that will help to:

- Clear any mental fog to strengthen your focus on what you really want (AIR)

- Purify and dance in the flames of your passions, to find your purpose and fulfill your potential (FIRE)

- Cleanse and dissolve those old wounds and move into your own abundant flow (WATER)

- Ground with the right action to manifest those riches (EARTH)

- Integrate and bind together every element in continuous motion (SPIRIT)

Witches are energy workers. When you work to balance the elements inside yourself and integrate them into your life, you embody the magic of your soul.

Why Abundance?

Some years ago, I wrote a chant for abundance:
Listen to the audio version here: **bit.ly/3XE0VJ7**

> *I am abundance*
> *I am prosperity*
> *The spirit of love and life is within me*
> *I see on every level*
> *I hear in every way*
> *The universe enriches me in all ways*

This has become my magical mantra and I offer it to you now. Inhale those words deeply and sing them often, because that is what you will experience in this book. The magic of abundance is going to flow through you like a river. You will be bursting with such vitality and vibrancy that your cup (Water nature) will runneth over into every area of your life. You will be creating magic that will *change your life*.

I'm assuming you want that? I thought so.

In *Riches for Witches* we are broadening our horizons, raising our sights and expanding in every direction for our highest good. Levelling UP.

Abundance has no room for lack or limitation. So whatever (you think) you are short of in life, be ready for the changes to come. I have been singing the Abundance Chant as a practice for some years now and it continues to work its magic on me still. But it has *not* happened overnight.

Instead, it's the result of intentional action that comes from a burning desire to create. To manifest. I believe in the power of the chant's words and in myself to act in harmony with them. And that is something required of you if you want to become prosperous and wealthy.

Self-reliance is the greatest magic.

So Who Am I to Tell You This?

I have been practicing Witchcraft both as part of a coven and as a solitary for over twenty years now, and during that time as a spiritual reader, healer, and teacher I have been holding space for others to access the intuitive guidance of their soul... what I call *the magical nature*. It is a complete privilege to be doing this kind of work.

As a singer-songwriter with Morrigans Path, I have come to know music and writing as a powerful form of magic, and I draw upon the bardic spirit in many of my practices to create abundance. It has not let me down.

Through these practices, I have created a life in which I work at doing what I love, supported by a loving husband and family. I'm not a millionaire, but I have many if not most of the things I want from life, and *I appreciate them every day*. I am abundant where it matters and I feel a living connection to the universe which I cherish deeply. Much of this comes down to the magical practices that I'm about to share with you.

I might add that I am not a finished product. I will always be a work in progress. Isn't that all any of us can be? One of the reasons for writing this book is so that I can continue to work magic on myself by helping you to do the same. There is no sugar-coated magical pill I'm afraid, but with real effort, and by embracing abundance on every level, you can fulfil your creative potential and manifest real change in your life.

How Is This Going to Work?

A magical life of abundance is being, doing, and having everything you need to create whatever you desire. There are no restrictions or barriers apart from the ones you create and allow within your own mind.

And this is not a new-age fancy. This is *old-age magic*.

It is the ongoing work of constantly checking in with yourself, correcting your course, and moving forwards. **YOU** are the work in progress creating and manifesting *all the time*.

The aim of alchemy, one of the most esoteric and mysterious of the magical arts, was to transmute the leaden nature of the lower self into the golden nature of the higher self. In *Riches for Witches*, the quest for gold continues, providing a course of study and practices for the modern-day Magician and Witch to create a life of abundance in every area of life.

The book is divided into three sections:

1. **DREAMING GOLD** – developing an abundant mindset and heart-set for the journey and transforming any self-worth issues into *self-wealth solutions*.

2. **DIGGING FOR GOLD** – diving deep into the work and investing your energy wisely.

3. **FINDING GOLD** – embracing riches, sustaining wealth, and sharing in your good fortune.

Terminology and Structure

As in *The Witch Wavelength*, I have kept the bones of the book the same. I want to clarify some of the ways in which I have used the English language and my own personal references throughout the book.

Firstly, I have capitalised Witch and Witchcraft (or the Craft) because I think they deserve the same respect as proper nouns relating to other spiritual traditions and religious paths.

Secondly, I have used the following words and terms interchangeably and sometimes in association with Witch, although it must be said not everyone who practises magic *is* a

Witch. However, we're on the witch wavelength here, where a less rigid perspective is helpful in terms of semantics.

The Magical Ones

- Witch
- Magician
- Shaman
- Sorcerer/ess
- Seer
- Wisdom Keeper
- Healer
- Wise Woman/Man

These are the walkers between the worlds of spirit and form, the seen and the unseen, the physical and the non-physical. How each individual does this will differ among traditions and paths, but the principle remains the same. The Magical Ones are co-creators with the sacred power of nature, skilled in ancient wisdom and magical craft.

My own perceptions of other interchangeable terms are:

The Magical Nature – Natural Wisdom – Soul Essence

The combination of Earth, Air, Fire, Water, and Spirit within us, form our magical nature. By tuning into the natural wisdom of our soul essence we blend each element to clear, purify, cleanse and ground our energy; preparing the way for change.

The Divine – Spirit – Source – The Universe

The purest form of spiritual life force, perceived as a holy and higher power.

The Gods – Angels – Ascended Masters – Spirit Guides – Ancestors

All those who reside in the eternal realms of spirit.
The human being is first and foremost a spiritual being. Every one of us is an eternal spirit moving beyond form and back to our spiritual home in between lives.

Magical Realms – Otherworld

The spiritual realms, but not necessarily the Underworld, as in the 'abode of the dead'.

Sacred

The divine embodiment of all creation. The earth and Her inhabitants are sacred. *We* are sacred. All of life in spirit and form is held in deep reverence, and honoured by the Magical Ones. Sacred power is our own natural wisdom vibrating at high power frequency!

Soul

The soul is the vehicle of our non-physical self, existing independently of the body. It's the spiritual blueprint that holds the sum of our parts from lifetime to lifetime. It is the divine and timeless part of who we are that animates our earthly body and leaves it at the time of death.

During the last week of my dear mum's life, I stayed with her and did what I could to help her pass peacefully. And when the time came I was comforted by knowing her soul was on its way home. On returning to my house in the early hours of the next morning, I was sitting quietly in the living room when I saw a heron taking flight from our back garden. That was all the confirmation I needed from spirit speaking through the magic of nature!

It is an incredible privilege to walk between the worlds. The soul is non-denominational. There is no belief system attached to it, although it is spoken about in all faiths. I see it as an intuitive expression of our creative spirit and magical self.

Create – Manifest

Used together or separately, to bring something into being with intentional action. Spiritual awareness infuses our minds and hearts with the presence of the sacred, creating and manifesting through us all the time.

Abundance – Prosperity – Wealth – Riches

Each has its own similar magical frequency on the witch wavelength. This book is an exploration of them all.

Mantra – Chant

A specific intention distilled into a short phrase to repeatedly think, say or sing. Mantra is a Sanskrit word for a sacred message or text, charm or spell. Chanting a mantra as a magical tool of transformation is very much a thread running through this book.

Thirdly, regarding gender, I have avoided using the generic feminine or masculine, and used 'they' or 'their' to indicate the indeterminate singular as well as plural. For example, *Once a Witch tunes in to their own magic, they empower themselves...* Female, male and non-binary people are all-inclusive within these pages.

Magic is for everyone.

WITCH WAYS

Within this section of each chapter, these are some of the practices to give you hands-on activities for your own prosperity.

- Spell work
- Mantra Magic
- Pathworking/Visualisation
- Witch Walking
- Divination
- Crafting

NOTE: To fully experience the magic for yourself, I recommend listening to the audio versions of the pathworkings, chants, songs and podcast episodes. All you need to do is type in the relevant bitly link to the browser on your digital device, and hey presto...

IN A NUTSHELL

Riches for Witches is a journey you will enjoy if you are willing to act on your intentions and do the work. With riches flooding our consciousness and influencing every thought, feeling and action, there is no limit to what we can achieve with the vibration of abundance. It is the boundless magic of life.

The wisdom of the natural world is here to guide us everywhere we look; in the heart of a candle flame and the ripple of a rolling wave, in a fresh wintry breeze, and in the musky scent of freshly dug earth.

And so we invite our friends and allies, the Gods and the ancestors, and all angelic beings and loving spirits from this world and the next to join us on our quest. What a great support team.

We begin the journey by tuning into your idea of personal riches, followed by the tools and practices of the work itself. And finally, you will learn how to sustain abundance and to keep creating it in your life.

Now that you get the picture, let's get started... there's magic to be done!

DREAMING GOLD

1
TUNING IN TO RICHES

The name of the game is the attunement to consciousness – Gareth Knight

Firstly, let's think about what a magical life of abundance looks like. What is your idea of riches? Here are some words to get those golden juices flowing:

- Happiness and health
- Wisdom and wealth
- Prosperity
- Financial freedom
- Affluence and success
- Generosity and plenty

Enjoy and savour the taste of each one of these golden nuggets. Can you think of any more? Write them down. Start to resonate with your own rich wavelength by grounding the energy in a physical act.

Tuning In

Turning an idea over in your mind is a good way to develop a contemplative practice for your magical work. I love to ponder over things, and the beauty of pondering is that you can do it anywhere, any time. You can do it while performing some monotonous task that doesn't require too much brain power, and let the mind toy with the idea, playing with it from every angle.

Do not underestimate the power of pondering. It's a very versatile practice and extremely useful for all kinds of witchery... so get practising.

TRY THIS:

- Write down or draw anything else you can think of to describe your personal idea of riches. What does that look like for you?

- If you have a set of tarot cards take out the Ace of Cups and prop it up on your altar or somewhere you can see it often. For me that will be on my desk, staring at me from above and reminding me every time I sit down to write that I am in the flow of good feelings. I am doing what feels good (we will look at the tarot as a magical tool in Chapter 7).

- Alternatively, if you have a chalice or a cup of some kind, place it somewhere visible and use the symbolism to attune to the flow of abundance in you.

- Ponder on the energy of your words, the card and the cup. What does it look like? What does it feel like? What does it sound like?

- Listen to the Abundance Chant here: **bit.ly/3XE0VJ7**
- Visualise abundance filling every cell of your body.
- Dance it out... feel it *moving* through you.

The experience of grounding the energy of abundance through the body by singing, writing, art and movement is how you begin to work your magic. You can do this by yourself or with other kindred spirits. It can be great fun to create abundance magic together!

Riches for Witches is the grail overflowing.

What are you going to fill your cup with?

Prosperity

I love the energy of this word. It's filled with treasure and is a great all-rounder when it comes to riches. To prosper is to flourish and succeed, thrive and enjoy good outcomes. Prosperity also extends to our health, including physical, emotional and spiritual well-being, as well as our finances.

But whatever aspect of riches we're looking at, it starts on the inside. Let's place it in the heart. A prosperous heart is full of love. Now, while that may seem obvious to you, think about it and feel into it. When we are truly in love we are overflowing with feelings and cannot stop ourselves from projecting them outwards. The object of our affection may be a person, animal, place or even an idea. Love knows no boundaries when it comes to who or what acts upon it.

It's all about our feelings. *Riches begin in the heart.*

Contemplate this. Savour the taste of riches as you dare to dream of what those riches are.

Will it be money? Will it be health? Will it be happiness? Will it be holidays and travel? Will it be the freedom to do what you love and be richly rewarded for it? Why not all of those things?

Keep digging deeper and the treasure you are seeking, the words you are looking for to shape the dream will become clearer. It might seem a little foggy to begin with but stay with it, and notice what might be getting in the way.

What causes the fog? What creates the obstacles that stop you from seeing and moving toward your visions and dreams? Many things, but ultimately they all boil down to one: *fear.* By developing a clear and open mind and heart, and with a burning desire to take the right action, you will get through the fog. Your magical nature is the awareness of your soul waiting to guide you through it.

The Prosperous Heart

Our Water nature represents the realm of the heart and our feelings. We must enter this space if we want to bring riches into our lives. We must find our flow, turn it on and move with it.

To be rich and truly prosper in every area of your life, if you can feel it and imagine it and believe that you are in fact already rich, then you can manifest abundance and enjoy the riches of the universe. It is not out of reach.

It is right here, right now, and it's time to experience that feeling of riches inside you.

WITCH WAYS
Heart Practice

- Place a hand on your physical heart and close your eyes.

- Become aware of the spiritual heart and the unlimited

amount of love it holds.

- Breathe deeply into the feeling of love without conditions, rules, or boundaries.

- See that love expanding in pink and green rays out to every organ and cell in your body.

- Feel it circulating and gently push it out away from your body and into the space around you.

- See the rays expanding and filling the building (if you're inside) and eventually into the open air.

- Watch the rays of your prosperous heart touch everything and everyone they come into contact with.

- Bathe in the pink and green rays, breathing love in and out for as long as you want to.

- Ground yourself afterward with some water and gentle stretches... making sure you are fully back in your body.

How do you feel? This is a simple but powerful practice. Do it as often as you can and it will calm and ground you.

Magic begins with the self, and the first thing it changes is you.

The Witch has an abundance of tools at their disposal to do this work. We have the tools of the cycles and the seasons for a start; working with the wheel of the year and the moon phases will tap into the big energies of solar and lunar magic. It's a wonderful place to begin, but like any other tool, it's only as good as the worker who uses it.

So where do we start? As you're reading this, there will be a particular moon phase and time of the year breathing magic into your life. Tune into it, whatever time or phase it may be; this will mean you may need to skip ahead to the Moon and Sun chapters (9 and 14). You may want to dip in and out at the appropriate time for you and that's okay. Do that if you want to. It makes perfect magical sense.

Early Choices

Ever since I was old enough to decide what I wanted to do as a vocation, I have worked at what I loved.

When I was fourteen and choosing my options at school with my heart set on working with horses as a career, a head-teacher and my parents tried to dissuade me, proclaiming: *You're never going to make any money working with horses!* I didn't listen, of course. No one was going to tell me what I couldn't do. Especially about something I loved as much as horses.

Fuelled by a fierce determination to prove the naysayers wrong, I managed to make a living out of working with horses and worked and trained hard to gain good qualifications as a teacher in my field. It was a career lasting for over thirty years and took me across the world, and I loved every minute of it.

I chose to work with horses because I couldn't afford one of my own. My parents were working-class and constantly squabbling over money. My dad spent it while my poor mum worried over it... there was never enough. Although my brother and I were well cared for, a pony was beyond what the family purse strings could stretch to. And it wasn't only that, the initial expense is only the beginning... horses are expensive animals to keep and care for. Livery, food, shoeing and vet bills alone are costly amounts. So for me, choosing to work with them was the next best thing.

I could have chosen to get a 'good' job that would afford me the money to buy and keep one myself; I certainly came across many people who did that. But it wasn't for me. I wanted all in, a fully immersive experience of living and breathing with those beautiful beasts and it was absolutely the right decision for me at the time.

But even though I made a living from horses and had some jobs where the wages were pretty good, I never managed to save much. In fact I was not good with money at all. It always seemed to slip through my fingers and although there was always enough, it never felt like it!

Conditioning

The point I want to make is, my early conditioning around money had an effect on me. My dad's careless attitude and my mum's constant worrying sowed seeds of fear which influenced my life and I grew up feeling there was never enough. When you have lived with the seeds of lack in an environment of worry and fear, your garden grows weeds rooted in those fears, and your relationship and behaviours with the cause of those fears becomes the norm.

Our early conditioning around money has a huge influence on how we conduct our affairs and relate to physical currency. If we are not aware of this, we play out the early programming that has secured itself deep into our subconscious and continues to control us. It's only when we become aware of this that we have the opportunity to change the course of our lives.

My parents are no longer around, and although I still do some teaching with horses, my main job now is writing, teaching and healing. I am proving not only to my parents but to my own children that it can be done in whatever vocation you choose.

You can do that too.

Reflection

Take a moment to reflect on your own upbringing around money, prosperity and abundance.

- What were the attitudes of your family regarding these things?
- How has your early conditioning influenced the way you deal with money in your life?
- How do you feel about it now?

Write down your answers and ponder on them...

IN A NUTSHELL

There's no doubt that our upbringing around abundance has a major impact on how we experience it throughout life. However, by tuning into your own idea of riches, you have created a magical frequency personal to you *now*. Not only have you pondered on what abundance means to you personally, but you have embodied it by bringing it through into the physical world. You have written it down, felt it in your heart, chanted and danced it out. The spirit of abundance grows inside you and enriches your life in all ways.

Your cup runneth over, Magical One.

2
WEALTHY WITCH

Wisdom is the path to wealth – Ayodeji Awosika

Wealth is the vehicle that helps you to manifest your dreams. There are no shortcuts. The magic of wealth lies in your ability to create long-term abundance and security. It also lies in your ability to have patience, because when you're focused on building wealth into your life, you know that you don't need everything to happen right away. You can take your time and learn the skills needed to build those foundations and create a solid base to work from.

Relax then, my friend, and let's think about how wealth can and does influence every area of our lives.

Health

When we are balanced and whole in mind and body, our energy is vibrant. We enjoy good health. Without a healthy mind and body, we are poor in spirit. When our health is out of balance it depletes our energy and drains us. *Our health is our wealth.*

Witches are in tune with the energetic fields around them and within them. We know how to adapt our energy to the environment by working with the magic of nature and the many forms of guidance from the invisible realms. We come to know from the wisdom of our own experiences that a healthy Witch *is* a wealthy Witch.

Relationships

When our relationships are balanced and healthy, we are wealthy because we value ourselves and each other. As a Witch, you will learn to develop a healthy relationship with yourself first and foremost because without valuing who you are, the skills and tools you use to work your magic will be useless.

As Witches and Magicians, we must prioritise our self-worth to enrich our magic in every way.

Creativity

Witches are *full* of creative energy. Magic seeks expression in so many ways and provides a wonderful outlet for our creative spirits. Our creativity naturally draws us toward what we love to do. Sharing our creations follows as a result of practising and working on them, even if it's only among our friends and family to start with.

Creativity makes us wealthy just as being healthy does. They are all connected. On all planes of existence – spiritual, mental, emotional and physical – our contribution to the world is through our creativity. It's our magic in action.

Money

Wealth in a material sense consists of all the resources we own that give us financial security, such as assets, inheritance and employment. In modern society, money is one of the most common means of measuring wealth. For that reason it's an emotional subject because of the power we allow it to have over us. Money is a tool that can be used for the *distribution* of wealth, but is not wealth itself.

However, when our relationship with money is a healthy one, when we are grounded and balanced in good practices, accountable for our spending, invested in our savings, and generous and wise in our exchanges... we are financially healthy.

Self Worth and Self Wealth

What kind of price tag do you put on yourself? How much do you value who and what you are?

All self-worth issues that you harbour in any shape or form will have an effect on how much abundance you allow into your life. I come across so many people in the spiritual field of work who have these very issues about how they value themselves, or rather, how they *don't* value themselves!

These are good people, skilled in their professions. These are people who have paid good money for the kind of training that has added value to who they are as a professional. And yet, when it comes to connecting the dots between themselves and the prices they put on their own products and services, there is a short circuit.

They undervalue themselves and what they do. Does this sound like you?

Anyone, regardless of what their bank account says, can be an underearner. It's a mindset. A self-imposed condition. And only by focusing on overcoming it, will you begin to earn what you deserve and live a richer life. Yes, *rich*. Get used to that word and be ready to work magic on yourself because that's what you're going to do. A magical life of abundance can be created.

Witch Walk for Wealth

Take a walk out in nature and pose your questions to the universe with the intention of receiving an answer. It will help to free your mind and untangle any mental knots getting in the way of your own natural wisdom. These are walls built by ways of thinking that have stopped you from receiving your abundance. The highest walls have been built on lack and limitation. Whatever we are focusing our attention on, we are putting faith in. When we are focusing on the absence of something we want, it will continue to elude us. *Worrying is faith going in the wrong direction.*
Whatever we want, convincing ourselves we don't have it, will stop it from coming anywhere near us as long as we beat the drum of negativity.

This is where one of our greatest tools, the imagination, can make all the difference.

What's Your Story?

We are natural storytellers. Most people love to tell stories about themselves and what has happened to them, and over the course of a lifetime, this becomes the story of their lives. Up until now, you have been telling yourself and others the story of your life through your conversations and self-talk.

What story have you been telling?

Everyone is telling some kind of story. Some people can turn the most mundane thing that has happened to them into a magical tale. My husband is a natural entertainer, which I'm sure is the result of performing in bands all his life. He has acquired the skill of reading and keeping the attention of an audience by entertaining them. Consequently, he is great company, which makes life good in many ways, apart from when I want someone to commiserate with. You can't have it all.

Ultimately, whatever story we have been telling ourselves (and others) becomes what we experience. We are creating and manifesting all the time. Whatever your story has been up until now, you can change it. But first, decide what kind of a story that's going to be.

What about a story of wealth and abundance? Can you imagine it? You are the author of your own life story, Magical One. Write it all down and hold nothing back. I dare you.

On the magical path, we have the tools and practices of our craft to work and shape the life we want. A life that enables us to heal and bring balance and power to ourselves and our creations. However, as a human being, the Witch is still vulnerable to the nature of the lower self; we do not easily escape the ogre of doubt, uncertainty and fear. As such, we are at the mercy of whatever self-image we have built from our beliefs about ourselves.

These are the beliefs that have evolved mostly at a subconscious level from the conditioning of our environments and upbringing. We are hard-wired from early programming in childhood, with thoughts, feelings and behaviours that influence and determine the direction of our lives. But everything changes when we realise the power of our own creativity. Magic can happen.

Witch Ways
A Pathworking With the Seer

Listen to the audio version: **bit.ly/3ptorLX**
Begin your connection to your inner magic with solitude and stillness. Close your eyes and turn inward... taking slow deep breaths to relax you.

- Focus on your contact with the ground... inhaling the earth's energy through the soles of your feet... and exhale out again... slowly.

- Imagine putting down roots of golden light into the earth, travelling deeper into the ground with every breath.

- You take in the earth's energy, feel it flowing around your body... filling every cell, and flowing like roots spreading... back into the earth.

- Imagine this circuit of golden light as it draws up from the earth, moves around your body, and flows out again with each breath... slowly and naturally... in and out.

- Connect to your magical self by engaging all your senses... and remember that what you see and hear, and what you smell and feel will add *power* to your experience... building the images around you as you go.

- Feel the energy flow increasing as you open your mind, sensing the freedom it gives you as you shift your focus from the outside world to the inner planes... and your third eye centre.

- Picture a doorway and walk through it.

On the other side is a path lit by the glow of a full moon... and you begin to follow it along fields and hedgerows; the scent of damp earth lingering in the air. You keep walking and finally reach an opening to an ancient wood filled with mighty oaks and silver birches. The hoot of an owl calls through the low branches. Leaves brush against your skin as you walk deeper into the wood, eventually coming upon a grove of oak trees bathed in moonlight.

Someone is standing in the middle. A tall woman dressed in a hooded cloak of feathers, looking down at the ground. You walk towards her and she looks up at you slowly, with a hint of a smile. You notice a string of bones and hag stones around her neck, and in one hand she holds a staff with symbols carved all around it, and a small leather pouch hanging halfway down.

And there, sitting calmly at her feet is a black shaggy dog flicking his tail to greet you.

'Come and join us,' she says. 'The moon will point the way...'

The grove is flooded in silvery light and all is quiet except for the owl calling between the trees. You can hear the sound of your own heartbeat thudding against your chest as the woman takes the pouch from her staff and shakes it from side to side before emptying its contents on the ground. A collection of small sticks tumble out, and in the spotlight of the moon you notice they are not sticks at all... but bones.

She chuckles as she watches your face.

'The earth will not harm you, dear soul. She is wise; she is all-knowing... *she sees you.* Let us sing over the bones, the song of the Mother together...'

MOTHERS CHANT ~ MORRIGANS PATH

As the song fades, the words stay with you and reverberate around your body, filling you with a power that grounds you deep into the roots of every tree in the grove... down into the earth.

'Ah you feel her now don't you?' says the woman. 'Under her skin is the wisdom of the earth... can you taste it?'

The woman speaks in riddles, and yet, you know what she is saying. She continues to talk as she looks at the ground, tracing the patterns of the bones with long fingers while the dog watches.

'Here is your past,' she begins, 'and the wisdom of hindsight. What does it teach you? To let go of every limiting thought that has held you back from your good. Hindsight brings you the tools to change all that has gone before... to look upon the conditions you lived under with kindness. Everyone did the best they could. *You* did the best you could.

Dig deep, dear soul... forgive what's been and gone. Release the ties and burdens of your past and leave it behind you.'

She continues to move her fingers over the bones.

'And here is *now*. The gift of the present moment... the precious jewel of understanding and insight. All that enriches your world is revealed to you: the bright idea, a light in the darkness showing you a better way. This magical you, this child of the Gods... this strong and powerful soul who creates their own destiny... is *you*. Know this, and you will understand the true meaning of success and the work you must do for it; the work that creates wealth.'

Now her fingers point to the bones further away.

'And what of the future? How will you shape this destiny of yours? Think of the artist who holds the beauty of her creation in her mind, and begins the work of hands and heart. What will you make with yours? What do you see?'

PAUSE FOR A FEW MINUTES

Gradually, you come back from your dream time in the grove, but there is no sign of the Seer and her dog. They have gone. All that remains is a small flame, the flickering of an idea forming in your mind.

- You begin to walk away from the trees as the moon lights your way back to the path and continues to guide you out of the wood, along the fields and hedgerows, until you find yourself at the door once again.

- You walk back through the door and into the room.

- Take a deep breath in and feel yourself back in the physical body. Take another deep breath in and feel yourself back in the physical body.

- Wriggle your fingers and toes, stretching gently if you need to.

- You are back in the room... back in your body and fully grounded.

Welcome back.
THE MAGIC IS DONE.

You can revisit the Seer's grove at any time and receive her guidance. When you connect to this magical being, your perception of time changes. The past, present and future merge to bring you the ageless wisdom of the earth, enabling you to see where you have been, where you are now, and where you are heading in life.

IN A NUTSHELL

When you tell the story of your own abundance, you open the door to riches and align yourself to wealth in all its forms. With the aid of hindsight and insight, you can develop the tools to shape your future, and develop the foresight needed for a life of riches *here and now*. Your work will pay off.

You are totally worthy of all the riches the universe has to offer. I have the utmost faith in your ability to create it.

Now you must believe it too.

3
Natural Abundance

The earth contains untold riches – Ernest Holmes

If you have difficulty imagining what abundance would look like in your life, then let's start with the magic of nature. I want you to take a look around you right now, wherever you are.

Look for abundance.

You won't have to look far. I can't see where you are but there's one thing I know; you're breathing in and out. You are alive and kicking. It's in the air you breathe. Think about that, take it in as you sit there and breathe in and out.

Is there enough air to go around? Of course there is. It's everywhere. It's inside you, it's flowing around you. There is an abundance of the stuff.

As you sit and ponder on this, feel your lungs and your thoughts expanding as you receive the flow of abundance from the air around you.

This is what abundance is. It's more than enough of everything you need. It's flowing towards you, giving you life. It's flowing away from you, giving life to others. You are sharing your abundance as it pours out and enriches all those it touches.

Are you feeling that? This is not some fluffy cloud you're floating around on with no ground in sight. This is grounding yourself in the idea, the feeling, the act of, and the manifestation of abundance with the one thing that we all have: our breath. This is before we add anything else into the mix.

A profoundly simple but powerful practice.

Something else you can do is go outside and find a patch of grass anywhere you like. A garden, a park or a field somewhere, and look at that grass. How many blades can you see? Please don't start counting; I won't see you again. But you get the idea. That's *abundance.*

Go walk on a beach and contemplate how many grains of sand there are, and how many spoonfuls of water are in that ocean. Look up at the sky at night and ponder on how many stars there are, whether you can see them or not. They're there, and you know it.

How amazing is all this? All around us in this magical creation we call the the universe, abundance is flowing. Look and look some more and you'll see it's never-ending. The birds, the trees, the leaves on the trees, plant life, animal life… we live in a bountiful and prosperous universe. We are part of it all.

We are human, spiritual *and* magical beings. If that's not abundance, I might have to eat my hat.

WITCH WAYS
Meeting the Grail Maiden

Listen to the audio version here: **bit.ly/3NLByBy**

Make your connection to your inner magic with solitude and stillness. Close your eyes and turn inward, taking slow deep breaths to relax you.

- Focus on your contact with the ground… inhaling the earth's energy through the soles of your feet… and exhaling slowly.

- Imagine putting down roots of golden light into the earth, travelling deeper into the ground with every breath.

- You take in the earth's energy; feel it flowing around your body... filling every cell, and flowing like roots spreading back into the earth.

- Imagine this circuit of golden light as it draws up from the earth, moves around your body, and flows out again with each breath... slowly and naturally... in and out.

- Connect to your magical self by engaging all your senses. Remember that what you see and hear and what you smell and feel will add *power* to your experience... building the images around you as you go.

- Feel the energy flow increasing as you open your mind... sensing the freedom it gives you as you shift your focus from the outside world to the inner planes... and the third eye centre.

- Visualise a doorway leading out of the room and walk through it, closing it behind you.

You can feel the softness of grass underfoot as you look down and see an overgrown path leading away from the door. You begin to follow it through fields of wildflowers and tall grasses growing in their masses. Blue cornflowers and white daisies scatter as if the faeries themselves had sprinkled them over the land.

You can feel the warm spring sunshine on your skin as you make your way along the path, enjoying the song of a skylark flying way overhead. You notice how the path begins to climb upwards, gradually becoming banked by large rocks. It takes you higher and finally, on reaching the top, you realise you are looking out over a steep drop where water is gushing and falling onto the rocks below into a bubbling spring.

The moment you look down at the waterfall, you find yourself standing under it in the warm waters of the spring. In the heat of the sun, the water is soothing. You tilt your head back, close your eyes and open your arms to the flow, letting it wash over you. It feels so good! And you are enjoying it so much, you stay there under the waterfall as it runs over your tired body... refreshing every pore and cleansing every cell with pure vibrant energy.

Eventually, you open your eyes and notice you are not alone. There's someone standing next to you... a young, golden-skinned woman in long white robes, golden hair tumbling around her bare shoulders. She beams a radiant smile at you and begins to speak:

'I am Maiden of the Grail and of this sacred spring... bringing you the magic of water to cleanse your mind and body... and to open your heart to the flow of abundance. Cleansing and healing, the flow of good feeling... Feel me as I flow through you, as I wash over you, as I pour out of you...'

With both hands she holds up a shining silver chalice, catching the water as it falls and spills over the sides, and begins to chant:

> *I am the well of all-knowing,*
> *within you a feeling*
> *Rising and surging, cleansing*
> *and healing*
> *I am the magic of plenty, inside*
> *you and growing*
> *Abundance within and without*
> *you is flowing*

The sweet sound of the Grail Maiden's voice runs over you like water, and she continues to pour from the silver chalice as the water from above fills it and runs over and over...

> *As above the power flows*
> *As below the magic grows*
> *As within the power seals*
> *As without the magic heals*
> *Pouring over from above*
> *The spirit of eternal love*

She stops chanting and speaks:
'Here, in this place, there is only now... a moment of magic. A feeling of pure potential to tend and nurture and grow. My water runs over and fills your cup... my love pours into your heart. The joy of plenty, the glow and vibrancy of good health, the certainty and assurance of wealth, the flow of abundance... this feeling, with you, here and now.

Feel it and allow it space to grow. Keep your mind and heart open, your hands ready to give and receive. I will show you how...'

The Maiden opens her arms wide, beams her radiant smile at you, and continues...

'You feel different because you know this is the power to change whatever you want. This is the magic at work, dear soul. Breathe it in and breathe it out... all your abundance flows from within. *All of it.* All your abundance flows from within.'

PAUSE FOR A FEW MINUTES

Coming back from your dreamtime, you look around to see that the Maiden has gone. You are standing alone beneath the waterfall, and you step carefully back onto the path and begin to walk home. You are tingling with renewed energy. You can feel it flowing and pulsing around your body in waves... you know it's changing you... and it feels *so* good!

- You gradually make your way down the hillside and back through the fields of wildflowers where the colours are brighter and the birds are singing sweeter than before. Nothing is the same. *You are not the same.*

- Following the path eventually leads you to the same familiar door and you walk back through it and into the room.

- Take a deep breath in and feel yourself back in the physical body. Take another deep breath and feel yourself back in the physical body.

- Wriggle your fingers and toes, stretching gently if you need to.

- You are back in the room... back in your body and fully grounded.

Welcome back.
THE MAGIC IS DONE.

Remember that you can return at any time to spend time with the Grail Maiden at her sacred spring. She will always welcome you with open arms and an open heart.

Corresponding Matters

Energy correspondences make up a multitude of categories that can add power to our magic. We employ these energies to align with particular elements: symbols, times and cycles, planetary activity, colours, stones, plants, deities, etc. which we *associate* with our desires and intentions. For our work with abundance, here are some examples of prosperity and success correspondences:

- **Colours** – red and orange for success/green for prosperity
- **Stones** – hag stones, clear quartz, green garnet, citrine, aventurine
- **Moon cycle** – new to waxing moon for prosperity/full moon for success
- **Sun cycle** – morning – mid-afternoon
- **Plants** – basil, blackberry, vervain, dill, cinnamon, clove
- **Oils** – myrrh, almond, saffron
- **Gods** – Lakshmi, Dagda, Rosmerta, Cernunnos, Oshun

Fundamentally, your own energy and belief in what you are doing is the most important element. If you don't have a specific colour candle at (what you think is) the right time, don't let it put you off. Your intention is what counts. Over time you will build up your own list of correspondences that have meaning and will work for you. For example, I find early mornings with a tealight and a bay leaf are a good time for me. I contemplate my intention, write a symbol on the bay leaf, burn it the next day and repeat. Remember, there is nothing that cannot be improvised to suit whatever spell you are casting or practice you are doing.

Believe in your own intuition, and it will serve you well.

In a Nutshell

The magic of nature in all its forms reminds you of the seeds of abundance growing inside you. Meanwhile, the Grail Maiden has left you with a feeling you will never forget. Keep her close to remind you of the feeling of abundance in your life… expanding every good thought and feeling you have.

Weaving the magic into the mundane is where the Witch really comes into their own. Experiencing the sacred in the ordinary and everyday life of being human is where our magical heart beats the loudest.

These are the riches of abundance in action all flowing from within.

4
THE POWER OF LOVING INTENTIONS

What you mean when you do a thing determines the outcome – Breanna Yovanoff

The power of your intentions activates your magical nature to weave each element together in co-creation with the cosmos. This is why understanding and appreciating what the elements do will keep you focused on your magical work with abundance. When you are able to blend and balance the spiritual essence of the elements within yourself, you are grounding your own unique soul nature into everyday life. You embody the power of the sacred.

- The magic of Air breathes life into the thoughts and ideas you have. How you plant the seed of your intentions is through the mind.

- The magic of Water flows through your emotions, connects you to love and nurtures the relationship with your intention.

- The magic of Fire brings purpose to your passions and forges the two to fulfill your creative potential. It's the picture you paint and the story you write to bring your magic to life. Fire is the alignment of thought and feeling with action.

- The magic of Earth is the result of that action. Manifestation is the alignment of your thoughts, feelings and actions mirrored back to you.

- The magic of Spirit is the love and life force that weaves its way through the elements and connects everything and everyone. It is the eternal essence of your infinite self, experienced through the power of your intentions, creating in every moment.

And since love is an absolute requirement for building an abundance consciousness, a heart-centred approach will help you do this.

The Wisdom of the Heart

The heart is literally your treasure chest of riches; your Water nature. All the dreams and desires you have for creating abundance in your life are held in this place. It's the storehouse of every loving feeling you have. When you love someone or *something* (e.g. a place, animals, music) with all your heart, that's where it lives, expressing through your mind-body connection as feelings, and manifesting through your intentions and actions.

The Old and the New

Science now confirms that heart intelligence influences our creativity and plays a major role in our health and happiness. Finally, it's catching up with ancient wisdom, which has been saying for centuries, that the deep magic of the heart has a direct and profound effect on our daily lives.

The spiritual traditions of Paganism and Druidry, Daoism, Sufism, Judaism, Hinduism, Buddhism, Native American, Aborigine, Mayan and many other indigenous cultures around the world all demonstrate the heart's wisdom in their teachings. It's nothing new, and as the old structures continue to break down between magic, religion and science, we can see that the divisions that have caused so much alienation in the past are narrowing. There is no doubt that the heart of humanity will continue to expand and fulfill its long-awaited destiny.

The Holistic Heart

Over the past thirty years, research in neurobiology has led to the discovery that the heart has many parallels to the brain. Founded by Doc Childre in California, HeartMath® is a system of self-regulation techniques for the heart, based on the scientific studies of stress, emotions and the interactions between the heart and the brain.

Here are some of the discoveries made in the research:

- The heart is comprised of 40,000 specialised neurons that can sense, feel, learn *and* remember, forming its own independent nervous system.

- The most powerful energy field generated by the body is the heart's electromagnetic field. It radiates at least five feet around the body and interacts with other heart fields.

- The core heart emotions of love, appreciation and compassion reduce the activity of the sympathetic (fight or flight) nervous system and increase the activity of the parasympathetic (rest and digest) nervous system.

- Positive emotional states have a balancing effect on the nervous system by strengthening immunity, enhancing hormonal function and improving brain function.

- Heart rhythms are mirrored in our emotional states. Negative emotions such as fear, anger, and hostility create disordered and irregular heart rate variability (time interval between heartbeats), while positive emotions create improved order in the heart's rhythms.

Isn't it amazing how this holistic approach to science reaffirms mostly what we know intuitively in our hearts *about* our hearts! However, the discovery of heart rhythms is not unsurprising. This fact alone is enough of a deterrent to encourage us to make some changes in our attitudes and behaviour.

Witch Ways
Heart Magic

It's time to stir up some love vibes. This is a great spell if you are lacking in anything, and will motivate you to become prosperous.

Take your time with it, enjoy the work... and it will pay off.

You will need:

- Time alone in a dedicated sacred space, e.g. at your altar or out in nature

- A crystal that you love (rose quartz, kunzite, morganite, and green or pink fluorite are stones that are good for heart work)

- A candle

- Pen and paper or journal

- Red ribbon
- Rose petals

WHAT TO DO:

- Light the candle if you are indoors. If you're outside, imagine a flame burning bright in your heart.
- Hold the crystal in your hand.
- Make your connection to your magical self through stillness and silence.
- Take three slow, deep breaths in... hold for as long as you can... and exhale fully.
- Breathe the energy of the stone into your heart and hold it there.
- Bring to mind a person or an animal in your life who you love, and think about how much you appreciate them. How thankful are you for their presence and the difference they make in your life?
- Write down and pour out your feelings onto the page. Hold these feelings in your heart.
- Now focus on something that you think you *lack*. What do you feel you don't have enough of? For example: good health, money, time, confidence or motivation.
- Imagine how you would feel if you had plenty of it in your life. How much of a difference would that make? Imagine that.
- Now transfer the love in your heart and the crystal to that particular thing.

- Pour out your feelings onto the page once again. Let your imagination take you wherever it wants to... and allow yourself to express the feeling of abundance in any way that comes. Continue to write, and if you feel like drawing a picture, do that as well.

- Once you've finished, sit quietly with your words and pictures in front of you.

- Place the rose petals inside the paper, fold it and wrap in red ribbon. Keep them on your altar for a lunar cycle and then burn them.

- Keep the crystal with you.

THE MAGIC IS DONE.

Let your heart guide you. Revisit and repeat any time you like and work with anything else (you think) you don't have enough of.

You can always turn lack into abundance with heart magic.

Manifesting With Music

Music is a powerful form of magic. I love to write songs as you know, and there is one I wrote a few years ago, that for me, embodies the feeling of manifesting our heart's desire. 'Not a Dream' is about sowing those seeds of magic to create what we want. I'm including the lyrics here because they are a powerful spell casting, and combined with the music, you can use the song to charge and send your own intentions out into the world:

Listen to the song here: **bit.ly/3Nl4NKd**

Not a Dream

*Paint a picture in your mind,
see the colours glow
Another place, another time
You can come and you can go...
To a land far away from here
In a feeling ever so near*

*A distant echo from the past
Can you hear it say?
The die is waiting to be cast
Magic always finds a way
In pots of gold and falling rain
Sunny spells are here again*

*It's not a dream if it makes you feel
Like waking up
Then it must be real
It's not a dream if it all comes true
What does it mean, what did you do?
What did you do to make it all come true?*

I see you drawing from above
The power in your hand
Now will you turn it into love
And watch it spill over the land
Through every word and every deed
Are the fruits of all your seeds

And so your dream will always find
Where it is meant to go
Another place, another time
No need to chase, no need to follow
You will make it real somehow
If you live it here and now

Play this song (as long as you like it!) often. You can sing it while gathering ingredients for your spell work and preparing your sacred space. Sing it out loud and make it your own. Absorb its magic and feel it in your heart.

Earth energy is the manifestation of our dreams. If we don't *do* anything about them they will remain a fantasy playing out in our heads. Castles in the air! How grateful we can be for our physical bodies and the ability to act out our intentions. I am writing these words to you with my hands, the healers we take so often for granted. You are holding this book in your hands, whether it is a paperback or an ebook on a digital device, *it's in your hands.* Think about that for a moment… your own riches are within your reach. They are not something far away or out of sight. You can see them, you can feel them, you are holding your abundance right here, now. How much do you appreciate what you can do with your hands?

You've guessed it… gratitude is a game-changer.

IN A NUTSHELL

Remember that as a Witch, if you are in tune with yourself, you do not just believe in magic... you live it and breathe it. You listen to the wisdom of your heart. You work it into your everyday life, weaving each thread with the intention of creating exactly what you focus on. This may sound much the same as anyone else who is determined to reach their goals... but for the magically minded, it *is* different.

We tune in to our heart's wisdom to transform and increase the power of our intentions all the time. This is how we turn the dream into a living reality.

Now let's move on to explore the territory of the practical dreamer.

5
THE PRACTICAL DREAMER

Dreams come in a size too big so that we may grow into them – Josie Bisse

As a Witch, one of the greatest tools you have is your imagination. It is the doorway to the realms of magic where *everything* is possible. The moment you step into that world, you are not limited by time, space or circumstance. This is the dimension you move into to shape and begin to manifest whatever you are dreaming about. Even if it all feels a bit unreal to start with, you *can* imagine it.

This is the territory of the practical dreamer.

When you believe in your ability to realise your dreams, you will see opportunities to make them happen. But if you don't believe in yourself, all you will see are obstacles. You close the door to magic. Practical dreaming is a fun and easy way to keep that door open and will help you to plant and nurture the seeds of prosperity in your mind.

The Burning Desire

Practical dreaming is having a vision of being able to see who and where you want to be and imagining it's already here, right now. The power of your imagination is mighty, but you'll see it when you *believe it!* That burning desire will literally fire up your imagination and get you moving. But remember, it starts on the inner planes.

This is where an exercise from *The Witch Wavelength* is worth repeating:

Connecting to Your Inner Flame

- Make a fire and settle yourself down in front of it or light a candle and place it in front of you.
- Watch the flame(s) and breathe deeply.
- Connect with the present moment and invite the spirit of Fire to be with you.
- Call in your burning desire and ask it to show you what purpose it has in your life.
- Ask what it will have you create.
- Hold the image in your mind and take it down into your solar plexus.
- Feel its power.
- Draw on its energy and send it to every cell in your body.
- Ask the inner flame to fill you with the courage to act.
- Ask it to burn away any dead wood blocking your creative path.
- See the barriers breaking down and feel your energy clearing as you merge with the flames.

- Bask in the glow of your desire; see the dream taking form and the action needed for your next step towards it.

- Give thanks to the spirit of Fire.

Imagining

You can do all kinds of things to develop a more active imagination. Reading is one of them. I always find immersing myself in a good story clears my head and gets my creative juices flowing! Watching a live performance or a good film or series is another way of filling the creative well for the same reason.

Be mindful of your consumer habits, though. They can get out of hand. It's easy to find ourselves stuck to a screen, whether it's our phones, computers or the TV. Much to my surprise, when I looked this up, I was glad to see that many people still continue to enjoy consuming non-digital media. It's good to know that for all the frenetic busyness of our modern-day lives, sanity prevails!

Natural Ways

Become aware of opportunities to rest your mind without relying on external stimuli; it will nudge the imagination into action. When you're waiting in line anywhere, or for the kettle to boil, or drinking a cuppa... see if you can do only that. Slip into the liminal space and resist the robotic urge to grab your phone, and give yourself those in-between moments back. They are the breathing space you hunger for, and fertile ground for your creations.

Other ways of opening up to the imagination are: playing, walking, meditating, going out in nature, listening to music... Are you noticing any similarities with the magical path? These are the natural and creative ways of the Witch.

Bear in mind that all the great leaders of business and finance, and the great artists, musicians, poets and writers became great through their developed *use* of creative imagination. It is a fundamental tuning instrument of the mind. Like anything, if you don't use it, it will wither and die. Imagination is one of your most precious gifts. Nurture it, and it will be your greatest ally.

Working Out Your Why

Once you are clear on what your dream is there's no need to try and work out how it's all going to happen. But you do need to ask yourself why you're doing this. Why do you want to become rich? Why are you reading this book? I'm assuming it's because you want to create a magical life of abundance: a life of financial freedom, successful and loving relationships, a prosperous and healthy body. A deeper and richer spiritual life.

Knowing your 'why' will help to keep your motivation high, that all-important energy that drives you to be and do all the things required for that dream. Here are some examples:

I would love...
- To enjoy good physical and mental health.
- To have successful and loving relationships.
- A rewarding and enjoyable career or hobby.
- To fulfill my creative potential.
- To live a rich, spiritual life.
- To have the financial freedom to travel the world when I want, how I want, and with who I want.

Now take some time to zoom in on each of these areas. Ponder on each one and ask yourself why in particular you are choosing abundance in that area. Allow your imagination to roam freely.

A Writing Practice

Next, write down everything that comes into your mind about why you're choosing each one. No editing. Don't try to work anything out. Write freely for about ten minutes. Avoid using any digital methods. Make sure you write longhand in a physical notebook or on paper and let the words flow.

This practice will reveal more about how you feel about riches than you thought. It will also highlight the important factors that make the difference between a fantasy that stays in your head and the manifestation of your dreams into a living reality. Once your imagination is stimulated, you will find the motivation to act comes naturally, if a little slowly to begin with.

As I've mentioned before, don't worry about the how-to for now. Give yourself the time to dream first; be patient, and trust in the process of the practice.

WITCH WAYS
A Dream Altar

Once you have written down your dreams, creating an altar specifically for them is both a practical and magical thing to do. It will ground your intentions into a sacred space and serve as a constant reminder at all times. Tangible objects that you can see and touch, listen to and smell will help to keep your dream alive in your mind and body.

Here are some ideas:

GOOD HEALTH & SELF-CARE

- Sunflowers, carnations or lavender
- A picture of a sacred well, spring or any beautiful scene in nature
- A blue or white healing candle
- An angel ornament
- A healing-specific oracle or the Sun tarot card
- A piece of amber to keep the auric body cleansed
- A healthy diet sheet or book
- A hag stone for protection
- Crystals that align to the chakras in your body:

1. **Root** – red jasper, bloodstone, black tourmaline

2. **Sacral** – orange carnelian, tiger's eye, orange calcite

3. **Solar Plexus** – citrine, yellow tourmaline, golden beryl

4. **Heart** – aventurine, rose quartz, watermelon tourmaline

5. **Throat** – azurite, turquoise, sodalite

6. **Brow** – iolite, lapis lazuli, shattuckite

7. **Crown** – amethyst, sugilite, spirit quartz

Successful & Loving Relationships

- Roses or tulips, dill or marjoram
- A rose quartz heart
- A love-specific oracle card, the Two of Cups or Ten of Cups tarot card
- A gold and silver candle
- Sun and moon ornaments or symbols
- Shells
- Two swan feathers
- God and Goddess ornament or picture
- A photo of your loved one(s)

Love incense

You will need:

- Dried rose petals, lavender, cinnamon sticks, myrrh resin
- Charcoal burning disk
- Mortar and pestle
- Heatproof container

What to do:

Mix together, light the charcoal, and add the mixture once it has turned white.

Rewarding Career or Job

- A red candle
- Basil plant or dried herb
- The Three of Pentacles tarot card
- A hag stone and a clear quartz stone
- Jasmine plant/oil/picture

Creative Potential

- An orange candle
- The Empress and the Star tarot cards
- Orange calcite, yellow fluorite or moonstone
- A piece of graphite/a pencil and a notepad
- Paints or a drawing pad
- A packet of seeds
- A picture or figurine of the Celtic Goddess Brigid
- A photo or drawing of a Labyrinth

Spiritual Development

- A purple candle
- The High Priestess and Hierophant tarot cards
- A piece of labradorite or selenite
- A favourite spiritual book
- Yoga mat
- Mala
- Crystal ball/runes/oracles
- Singing bowl

Financial Freedom

- A green candle
- Three coins
- The Eight and Nine of Pentacles tarot cards
- A picture of an intended travel location
- A piece of citrine, aventurine or moss agate
- A money plant
- Your purse or wallet
- A business or promotional plan
- Money incense (see Chapter 19)

- A magnet

- A piggy bank

- Basil plant or dried herb

- A picture, oracle card or figurine of the Hindu Goddess Lakshmi

These are some ideas to get you started. Be as creative as you like with your own. For example, you could add your favourite fruit to a good health altar, or a gym membership card! My husband recently brought back a gorgeous lump of graphite from the beach, which is now sitting on my creativity altar (aka my desk).

Use what you have around you and add any objects for the elements: e.g. feathers and incense for Air and the mind, shells for Water and love, candles for Fire, and stones/plants/herbs for Earth and the body.

Chances are you will already have done that quite naturally. Whenever I create an altar, it always includes feathers, stones, shells and a candle of some kind. And remember, everything is a *representation* of your thoughts. It doesn't matter if you don't have the 'right' coloured candle... a tea light will do with the right intention behind it.

Symbolism is the language of the Witch. Use it to talk to the Gods... and they will hear you.

Turning the Mundane into the Magical

Practical dreaming is about integrating the spiritual into everyday life. Witchcraft is a practice, after all, and the more you can weave the magical into your daily routine, the better. Magic is as much a natural part of the Witch's life as breathing, and not only for sabbats, full moons, and spell requirements.

It's not so much about *what* we spend our time doing but *how* we go about it that makes the difference.

The Power of a Mantra/Chant

For example, when doing those all-important household jobs, working with a mantra can turn the monotony into something magical and *useful*. I know how hard it can be to reprogram all the negative thought patterns built up over a lifetime, but it can be done! And in my experience, working with musical mantras is one of the most useful ways of doing it. I don't know about you but I have never been able to stare in the mirror and repeat affirmations in parrot fashion... it all feels ridiculous to me. But singing them out feels much better.

Remember that the subconscious can't tell the difference between an impression that's real or not. Unless the conscious mind rejects it, the subconscious mind will accept whatever it receives, and that's how a program is created. Becoming conscious of what we are thinking is to take charge of these programs by changing them where necessary.

We can be the magicians of our own lives.

Creating a mantra, adding a melody and chanting your way through a mundane activity will transform your energy. It will raise your vibration. It will bring magic to your work at any level, even when you are staring at the bottom of a toilet. Try it.

Practical dreaming is the ability to hold that vision, regardless of your circumstances and conditions, and trick your subconscious into believing that it's *already here*. You can do it while walking or driving or indeed *anything you like*. But chanting is the perfect way to do it, as repetition is the key factor.

This is a simple but powerful mantra to work magic on yourself at any time. Listen to the audio version of Wholeness Chant here: **bit.ly/3qqVIxm**

You can create abundance in your life with the simplest of magical acts. This is sowing the seeds of success, one seed at a time.

Pathworking

The ancient art of pathworking is probably better known today (or at least in the last thirty years) as 'guided meditation'. Our ancestors and those who walked the paths of the mysteries knew only too well the power within them. It's a powerful technique and it works like a magic key, unlocking the doors of the mind with the imagination, to create and enter a world which can be just as real for us if we are willing to *do the work*. But this work requires skill, practice and discipline if we are to truly benefit from its hidden powers. If we don't bother to do the groundwork then the power will stay hidden and the work will have no value.

Pathworking is not just about visualising and watching a scene unfold before us, but about learning to step into the image and become a part of it on every level of our being. If we can train ourselves to develop acute sensory perception, if we can use our powers of observation to combine with the concentration of focused, mental energy, then pathworking can be a valuable tool for magical work.

It is said that we only use a fraction of our brains' potential, and as a result, much of its ability is never utilised. By enriching our minds we can build a data bank of images that we can draw on for our inner work. If we observe, study and practise using our imagination then we can use it to become healthy and empowered individuals. We can access knowledge, develop confidence and fulfil our potential as creative souls. We are going to use the power of the imagination to create something real. What becomes real for the mind – if given enough power – will move into physical reality.

It will manifest in our lives. It will have no choice but to follow the path of within to without.

Pathworking to Access Your Magical Nature

Listen to the audio version here: **bit.ly/44zGLlN**

Make your connection to your inner magic with solitude and stillness. Close your eyes and turn inward, taking slow deep breaths to relax you.

- Focus on your contact with the ground… inhaling the earth's energy through the soles of your feet… and exhale out again slowly.

- Imagine putting down roots of golden light into the earth, traveling deeper into the ground with every breath.

- You take in the earth's energy, and feel it flowing around your body, filling every cell and flowing like roots spreading back into the earth.

- Imagine this circuit of golden light as it draws up from the earth, moves around your body, and flows out again with each breath… slowly and naturally… in and out.

- Connect to your magical self by engaging all your senses. Remember that what you see and hear and what you smell and feel will add *power* to your experience… building the images around you as you go.

- Feel the energy flow increasing as you open your mind, sensing the freedom it gives you as you shift your focus from the outside world to the inner planes and your third eye centre.

- Close your eyes and place a hand on your heart.

- Say this to yourself:
  I am infinite and universal
  I am magical and eternal

Visualise a doorway leading out of the room and walk through it, closing it behind you. As you walk through the door you find yourself on a path. Follow the path as it meanders across fields and takes you into a wood. The sun is streaming through the openings in the trees and lighting up the path as it carries on through the wood and out into a clearing.

You find yourself at the foot of a mountain and continue as the path leads you around and up to the top. As you reach the mountain top you notice that the air is different, clearer. Feeling the grass beneath your feet, you breathe in the air and look around you. The scene is breathtaking and you know you are part of this.

With outstretched arms, you connect with the great Mother of Nature, the Goddess of all life. You feel her draw closer as you bring down the light from the highest realms, grounding it into your body. *As above, so below...*

EARTH CHANT ~ MORRIGANS PATH

Feel the light radiate within as it pulsates through every cell; replacing imbalance with wholeness, lack with abundance, and any discord with harmony and peace. Feel the light energy nourishing every atom at the very deepest level of your being.

Now focus on that energy and push it outwards and into the world around you. See it shooting out from your body in laser streaks of lightning and filling the space beyond. See it expanding and pulsating out into the universe. *As within, so without...*

This is the power of your own natural wisdom – the magic of Air, a clear and open mind... the magic of Fire, your creative potential... the magic of Water, an open and loving heart... and the magic of Earth, the process of manifestation, the answered prayer, the wish fulfilled... the dream realised.

This is your magical nature. Can you see it? Can you hear it? *Can you feel it?*

PAUSE FOR A FEW MINUTES

Returning from your dream, your whole body is charged with energy, your mind is clearer and your body wants to move!

Taking off, you follow the path around and down the mountainside. You enter the wood once more and continue following the path out across the fields where it eventually leads you to the same familiar door.

You walk back through it and into the room.

- Breathing deeply from the ground upwards, bring your attention to the physical body once more. Breathing deeply from the ground upwards, bring your attention to the physical body.

- Slowly bringing yourself back into the body, begin to wriggle your fingers and toes, stretch if you need to... and when you're ready open your eyes.

You are rooted and grounded. You are empowered and charged with the seeds of your own unlimited and magical potential.

Welcome back.

THE MAGIC IS DONE.

Witch Walking

The purpose of Witch Walking is to use movement to focus and send out your intention, and to receive guidance when you need it. As I mentioned above, you can work this into your household chores, or you can go out for a physical walk and weave the magic into every step.

I wrote about Witch Walking in *The Witch Wavelength*, and it's a great practice for everyday magic. While using rhythm and pace with the additional use of your voice, whether you chant or sing, you have a powerful tool for working your magic in any way you want to.

Here's a specific chant for riches:

> *I think act and grow rich,*
> *I think act and grow rich,*
> *I think act and grow rich,*
> *I'm a use-all-I-know Witch!*
> *I'm a reap-what-I-sow Witch!*
> *I'm a go-with-the-flow Witch!*
> *I'm a rise-up-and-grow Witch!*

This particular chant is great for getting into a groove while you're walking or doing the housework. Say or sing it out loud and build it into your own practice.

Have fun with it, bang a drum or tambourine, rattle a musical egg or something similar and dance out your intention!

With walking, singing and dancing, you can change your consciousness. You can alter your mindset and direct it anywhere you want it to go... to travel into the Otherworld and meet those guiding spirits who are waiting to help you.

Traditionally, this is how the Shamans and Witches of old would enter into the spirit realms for guidance and healing.

IN A NUTSHELL

Once you are clear on why you want to bring riches into your life, you will have an incentive that will motivate you to do the necessary work.

Setting up an altar, pathworking and Witch Walking are all ways of transforming your dreams into a living reality. They are practical ways of working your magic. With a specific intention, you can do it too.

Whether you're walking out in nature or working around the house with a vacuum cleaner, you can chant, sing or dance your way to riches, and enjoy yourself while you're doing it!

Next, we turn inwards and learn how to access spiritual guidance when we need it most.

6
CALLING IN THE MASTERS

Take one step toward the Gods... and they will take ten steps toward you – Joseph Campbell

In Napoleon Hill's evergreen classic, *Think and Grow Rich*, the author describes an imaginary council meeting with 'invisible counsellors' which he held on a regular basis. He chose nine men who'd passed to spirit whom he held in high esteem. Every night, over a long period of years, before going to sleep he would imagine this group of men seated around a table, with the sole purpose of rebuilding his own character so that it would represent a combination of the great men's characters he shared time with.

Hill would appoint himself as chairman and address every council member, asking for the knowledge he wished each to contribute. And they would all respond in characteristic ways and communicate with Hill as well as each other. Among them were the spirits of Napoleon, Ralph Waldo Emerson, Abraham Lincoln and Andrew Carnegie.

It's a fascinating account of someone who realised early on in life he had to overcome the handicap of birth in an environment of ignorance and superstition. Hill described himself as an 'earnest student of psychology' and assigned himself the task of 'voluntary rebirth' through this method of a spiritual council.

'The coordination of knowledge and effort between two or more people who work towards a definite purpose in a spirit of harmony...' is the mastermind principle that Hill coined. And the fact that he performed this act over many years is a testament to his dedication and commitment to this work in particular.

This was his own personal development work and building of character with all the qualities he aspired to for success, and he did it with the best minds and spirits for the job. And for that reason alone, Napoleon Hill, bless his heart, is definitely one of the members of my own spiritual mastermind group.

We are going to do something similar to tune in to working with our own helping spirits, to develop a spiritual network of support throughout our work to become rich on every level. So if you have been feeling on your own with this, know that you definitely are *not*. There is an abundance of spiritual help and assistance always available to you, waiting for the signal to draw closer, to make themselves known. And, as usual, we must remind ourselves that *success is in the preparation*.

So let's get ourselves ready to meet these magical masters.

WITCH WAYS
Creating a Magical Mastermind

It's time to fine-tune your wavelength to the vibrational frequency that aligns with your intention. In terms of energy, we have to raise our dense and physical vibration to meet the energy of Spirit. We have to meet them at their own level of existence, as the likelihood of them manifesting in a blinding flash of light – which would be amazing and wonderful – is, let's face it, a rarity. But that's not to discount the likelihood of it happening. We see it when we believe it.

What?

In our spiritual work, one of the most useful ways of doing this is to create a container for the magic to happen. And we do this most effectively through the act of ritual and ceremony: by creating room for the sacred between the boundaries of time and space.

Ceremony sets up the forces of nature to collaborate with us. It creates a bridge between the worlds of the seen and the unseen, providing a space where we can walk among them. It's a powerful tool to connect with the sacred. In this case, it's our mastermind group.

Where?

Entering from one place to another is easier to do when we can find a threshold to cross. In order to step away from the mundane, everyday reality and into the magical, a liminal space is required. Out in nature is ideal but not essential. A space indoors will do the job just as well, but as far as I'm concerned, nothing beats being out in the elements! I love to stand on the shoreline of the beach where I live, and there on the edge, feel the connection between land, sea and sky.

When?

How often we work with Spirit is entirely up to us. But when we have a job to do, questions to ask and guidance to seek we can usually feel the energy pull us towards the spiritual realms. Thought is potent, and as soon as you have the idea to set up your group, that sends out the vibration that connects you to the minds of those you are seeking.

And so the collaboration between your spirit friends and yourself begins...

Who?

Now comes the fun part. Take a pen and paper and write down your favourite personalities who have made an impression on you in some way. This can be anyone who lived an earthly life from any time in history... Spend some time on this and really think about it. Search your mind, your bookshelves, and your browser, and contemplate who you would like to meet in your mastermind group. Who are the successful people you have looked up to and would love to spend time with? If there is anyone who could share their secrets of success with you, who would it be and what would you like to learn from them?

Think about people whose genius, originality, talents, worldview and skills you have admired. All minds are available and are waiting and willing to share with you. No one is out of bounds!

Think about why you have chosen each spirit. What are the qualities they possess that you want to emulate and develop in yourself? Think about *abundance*. Ponder on what qualities and traits of character you will need to become rich on every level of your being... mind, body, spirit *and* pocket.

Write them down and contemplate the strength of their characters and exactly what you want each one to do for you.

I'm going to share mine with you as an example, and you can work with them if you like. I like to think that Spirit is omnipresent and available to all, plus it will give you an idea of the process.

- Napoleon Hill
- Stuart Wilde
- Wayne Dyer
- David Bowie

- Boudicca

Now we are going to gather these spirits together and open up the portal to the unseen worlds and meet our chosen ones.

Sacred Space

Performing a ceremony, whether it's a circle casting or simply lighting a candle, creates a bridge between the world of the seen and the unseen. Again, it's the intention behind it that makes all the difference.

Of course, there are potent times to perform ceremonies, based on moon phases, cycles, seasons and planetary aspects. But it doesn't matter what the planets are doing as you read this; play with the idea now and put it into action. There is nothing wrong with being spontaneous in your witchery and working magic as the need arises. I often sing or call into the wind to release or draw energy to me.

Natural magic is about being in the moment and harmonising with the powers of nature, and our connection deepens every time we do.

Letting Go

Firstly, release any personal energy that is standing in your way of success. Any thoughts, feelings and habits which are stopping you from prospering. Don't spend a lot of time on this, and think of a word for it. I suggest *past* is a good word to describe this energy. We cannot create a new future while still thinking and feeling like we've always done. It's time to *recreate*.

Write the names of your chosen spirit guides on a piece of paper or on a business card, preferably your own if you have one. You mean business and this is the power you want to work with. Embrace the power and open yourself up to the idea of a spiritual income and what that means to you.

Outside

Set your intention on a Witch Walk.

Go out in nature, where there is only yourself and the elements around you. Take your list of spirit guides with you and commit them to one of the elements. You can either:

- Bury the list in the earth to ground your intention for the group.

- Burn the list to keep the fires of inspiration glowing.

- Cast the list out upon an ebbing tide to stay in the flow of prosperity.

- Blow out your intention in bubbles, or say or sing each name out loud and let the wind carry and hold them.

For an extra boost, you can also combine all the elements by saying or singing (Air) each name into a hag stone (Earth) and casting out onto an ebbing tide (Water) during the day with the sun (Fire) overhead.

Outside is really one of the best ways to work magic because you are closer to the natural sources of energy. The elements are all around you, even if you can't see them. Remember, on a cloudy day the sun is up there shining, just as there is water in the clouds above or below on a dew-covered blade of grass. The magic of nature is abundant *everywhere you look*.

Speak your intention as described below.

Inside

Create your sacred space with an altar dedicated to your magical mastermind.

- Gather any relevant symbols, oracle cards, photos or pictures of the group, ornaments and natural objects, e.g. feathers, stones, shells and driftwood.
- Place your written list in the centre of the altar.
- Light a candle and speak your intention to the group:

> *Welcome each and all of you*
> *To help me with the work I do*
> *To think and feel, act and grow rich*
> *To be an abundant and prosperous Witch!*
> *I thank you for sharing here with me*
> *Your time, wisdom and clarity*
> *That I may benefit in every way*
> *Becoming richer every day*
> *By the power of the moon and sun*
> *With love to all and harm to none*
> *So mote it be!*

This is your call out, your *invitation* to the Gods.
Now it's time to settle yourself down and make yourself comfortable, ready to meet the magical masters. Remember that these are my own chosen advisors. Try this example first, to get a feel for it, and afterwards, you can create your own magical council in the same way.

A Magical Mastermind Pathworking

Listen to the audio version here: **bit.ly/43Uyxo1**

Make your connection to your inner magic with **solitude** and **stillness**. Close your eyes and turn inward, Taking slow deep breaths to relax you.

- Allow any tension to flow out of your body and back to the earth through the soles of your feet.

- Place a hand on your heart and take three slow, deep breaths.

- Be present... here and now.

- Focus your attention on your heart centre.

- Say to yourself:
  I am infinite and universal
  I am magical and eternal

- Connect to your magical self by engaging all your senses. Remembering that what you see and hear and what you smell and feel will add power to your experience... building the images around you as you go.

- Turn within and focus on the third eye centre.

- Visualise a doorway leading out of the room. As you walk through the door you find yourself on a path.

It's a warm evening. You look up to see a starlit sky and the bright glow of a full moon rising between the trees in the distance. You begin to follow the path. Running alongside the path is a stream and the water gurgles gently as the moon catches the ripples on the surface, dancing back and forth. You hear the low hooting of an owl ahead and breathe in the earthy scent of the damp night air from the fields. The path is soft underfoot and begins to climb up and around a hill bathed in the moonlight.

As you climb you notice a large stone building, standing on top of the hill, and you walk up to it slowly. The owl hoots again, welcoming you to the stone building, under an indigo backdrop of a starry sky. You continue to approach a large oval-shaped wooden door with a shining brass knocker... and hesitating at first, you knock loudly and wait.

After some time, while you wonder if you should knock again, the door begins to creak open and there standing in front of you in the flesh, is Napoleon Hill.

'Come in. We're expecting you!' he says, standing back to open the door wider, beaming a smile in your direction.

You follow Napoleon into the stone building where he leads the way through a narrow hallway lit with flaming torches. The flagstone floor is cold underfoot, and you can feel a cool rush of air around you.

At the end of the hallway, is a wooden door with a bright golden symbol on it. You take a closer look to see that it's a cornucopia filled with acorns and oak leaves, golden corn and coins spilling out of it.

Your leader pushes open the door and stands back to let you in. A winding stone stairway is on the other side and you follow him down the uneven steps, breathing in the heavy scent of musk in the air.

Down you go, placing your trust in your guide as you venture deeper into the unknown territory, until eventually you reach the bottom where the yellow glow of candlelight seeps out from beneath the door.

Your guide turns to you and says with a grin, 'Are you ready to meet the gang? They're all waiting!'

'I am,' you say, suddenly feeling your stomach flip.

He nods and smiles, 'Come in, my dear, and sit down...'

'We won't bite!' comes a loud chuckle, and you cast your gaze around the room to see who is talking. It's Stuart Wilde, leaning back on a chair with a glass in his hand.

He takes a swig of the golden liquid and beams a twinkly smile at you. 'Come on, do as the old boy says and have a seat.' He pats the empty chair next to him and you walk over and sit down and look around you, hardly believing your eyes.

You are one of many seated around an old and large round table, and can feel many pairs of eyes on you.

David Bowie is directly opposite you, leaning back on his chair, softly strumming a red acoustic guitar. 'No need for nerves, dear soul. It was you, after all, who called in the troops!' And he continues to play and begins to sing…the haunting melody of *Star Man's* familiar chords filling the room.

You are speechless, just sitting there staring at Bowie, this genius artist who you've loved all of your life. And now he is as close to you as an old friend, *talking* to you like an old friend and singing one of your favourite songs… *his* songs. Can it be real? Can any of it be real?

'So, here we are,' says a woman's haughty voice to your right, 'and here you are, indeed!'

You turn to see a flashing green-eyed Boudicca tossing her tawny plaited locks over one shoulder and resting one hand on her thigh.

'Quite the warrior aren't you? You need to be brave-hearted if you're going to triumph on the battlefield. What demons will you slay? And where is your sword?!' She throws her head back and lets out a deep cackle.

'Do not let the flame-haired one feed your fears, my dear.' It's the calming tones of Wayne Dyer. 'We're not all bad.' He slides a glance at Boudicca. 'Tell us why you're here… and what we can do to help you?'

'She needs to face her demons before anything else!' Boudicca's voice booms across the table, and she holds aloft a shining sword, glinting silver in the dimly lit room. 'You will need this to prune and cut away the dross from your life. There's no room for dead wood when you are growing rich! Take it and learn how to use it, and then you can have your shield... but not before!'

You stare at the great sword lying on the table and hesitate before placing both hands underneath it to lift it up. It's heavier than it looks, and as you bring it closer, you can hear the pounding of hooves and the cries of the battlefield all around you.

WARRIOR QUEEN ~ MORRIGANS PATH

As you ponder on Boudicca's bold words, the battle scene around you begins to fade... and you find yourself outside the building and back on the path heading down the hillside.

You follow the path alongside the stream in the moonlight to the sound of the owl hooting overhead. The scent of the damp meadows rises up from the ground... and the stream gurgles as you catch the moon's reflection in it.

Eventually, you're at the door and step through it, back into the room.

- Take a deep breath in and feel yourself back in the physical body. Take another deep breath and feel yourself back in the physical body.

- Wriggling your fingers and toes, stretching gently if you need to, and open your eyes.

- You are back in the room... back in your body and fully grounded.

Welcome back.
THE MAGIC IS DONE.

You can return at any time. Using this pathworking as a template, get to work and create your own unique mastermind group of chosen individuals. Try to make it a regular thing if you can and remember that building a relationship with anyone, alive *or* dead, requires time and commitment. Write your questions down and have them ready for each meeting. Record your findings and slowly but surely your masterminds will make their presence known and guidance will filter through. There is great value in this practice.

IN A NUTSHELL

Working on the spiritual level is the key to growth in all aspects of your life. For your world to change on the outside, you have to shape, mould and create from the inside. You have to work in the unseen and invisible realms in order to manifest in the visible realms.

You will find this easier to do in a ritual setting with physical symbols and tangible objects around you. It becomes an act of magic where the focus of your intention is to create the right conditions for a strong connection between yourself and the guiding spirits.

Remember to thank them always. Theirs is a commitment requiring much energy and a great love for humanity, and you will be all the richer for it.

7
TAROT FOR SUCCESS

It is not enough to depict things as they are –
Rachel Pollack

Having been a tarot lover all my life, it gives me great pleasure to include one of my favourite tools in our work together.

The tarot has many uses. Its main job is to guide and lead us to a greater understanding of our world and how we live our lives. Because the language of the tarot is in picture form and because of its ancient symbolism, it resonates deep beneath the surface of our subconscious mind. This plastic mold of mental substance is impressionable and a powerful and potent source of our energy.

It responds with ease to images because one of the main functions of the mind is to picture, to imagine all the time. It is constantly being programmed by all kinds of sensory input, most of which is on a subconscious level we are unaware of.

Therefore, with a visual tool like the tarot and its rich and diverse language, we can program it any way we like at a conscious level. We can plant seeds in our subconscious, literally molding the grey matter to suit a purpose, and it will affect us profoundly.

To help promote growth and success in our lives, a layout of specific cards will serve as a visual reminder and keep us on track with our purpose and focused on what we want. It is completely our choice what cards we use and this is the wonderful thing about the tarot – we can tailor it to suit our needs.

Success Spread

This is a spread specifically for success. This is a subject we all view differently but I believe that true success is a state of *consciousness*. It cannot help but reach out beyond itself and enrich all those it touches. It gives us freedom from all restrictions, allowing us to move and expand in whatever area or way we choose.

One of these areas is money, and that is why success is often associated with the acquisition of wealth. There is no doubt that money is important to us; we need it to survive in the world. Being subject at all times to the law of attraction, it makes good sense to prepare as much as we can for the reception of good fortune in our lives, and this is where the tarot comes into play.

The Sun

Central to our spread is the Sun, the bringer of success and the lighter of paths. Its radiance keeps us cheerful and optimistic, shining rays of life-giving energy on our chosen purpose. It helps us grow, gives us the confidence we need to move ahead and provides us with a consistent impression of increase.

Ace of Swords

To help us stay centred and clarify our minds is the Ace of Swords – the carrier of truth and integrity. To be successful, we need to make the right decisions. By cutting away all mental obstacles, we clear the way to move forwards with assertiveness and confidence. A strong sense of self-belief is a great motivator.

Ten of Pentacles

The Ten of Pentacles is a reminder that our success is rarely solely individual, comprising our family, friends and the community at large. The more people it benefits, the greater it is and the more permanent it becomes.

King of Wands

In the King of Wands, we find a true leader and generator of change. His innovative business skills, magnetic personality and ability to spot a golden opportunity are all abilities we can acquire if we apply ourselves. Developing and using the power to manifest a strong vision comes with his help.

Six of Wands

The Six of Wands brings us victory and triumph, particularly in business. This is recognition of a job well done and signifies the harnessing of passion to inspire others. Success comes all the sweeter for being well-earned!

Three of Cups

Finally, we have the Three of Cups to celebrate our achievements with our friends and family. Our goal has been fulfilled and our cup runs over with joy, keeping us open to inspiration and new opportunities. Here we are sharing our fortune with others, grateful for the good we have received and staying in the flow of magical abundance.

Working with the Cards

Setting out your cards in this way and using it as a focus for contemplation or meditation will serve as a reminder and keep the idea of success anchored in your subconscious. Growth accelerates during this period of incubation. It's a time of waiting and requires trusting in what you cannot see until it becomes visible.

This is an act of faith. There are many who give up at this point and the very nature of the downward, negative pattern of thinking will cancel out all the good. Keep onwards and upwards. Stick with it. Be patient and don't strain or worry.

Remember that all work on the inner planes eventually breaks through to the outer planes. Once the idea has taken root, it will grow as long as you give it the right conditions and continue to develop your intuition and act on it. *Use those cards!*

If you have more than one deck, it certainly helps. Keep your eyes on your Success spread – stick it on a board, put it on your altar or hang it up somewhere and look at it often. Pay it as much attention as possible, remembering that what we give our attention to... grows. And where we place our *intention*... it transforms!

Allow the creative power to work its way through the card energies and your pictured desire is certain of accomplishment.

WITCH WAYS
The Quantum Leap Tarot Spell

Take the Fool and the World from your deck and contemplate their magic in relation to your vision.

The Fool

Here is the great magical adventurer representing you at the start of your road to riches... symbolising the willingness to take a leap of faith and begin the journey. This is you trusting in yourself to change what you need to, to move forward and follow that dream.

The Fool's magical mantra is: *I take a leap willingly.*

On our quest for gold, let's tailor-make that to: *I am willing to believe that abundance is really possible.*

This will open you up to the spirit of the idea on every level.

The World

Here you are having completed your journey. It symbolises success and celebration; and reaching a well-earned goal. This is you reaching your goal of enrichment in every aspect of your life with a sense of fulfilment and balance.

The World's mantra is: *All is whole and complete in my life.*

Let's tailor-make it to: *I celebrate my abundance of happiness, health, wisdom and wealth.*

WHAT TO DO:

- Place the Fool and the World on your altar.

- The Fool is the beginning of your plan. Where are you heading, and what do you believe you want to achieve?

- The World is your goal already achieved and your intention made manifest.

- Keep on your altar for one lunar cycle.
- Light a candle each day to honour the magic and allow it to happen as it will.
- Act on the guidance as it comes, which it will.

Improvisation

You can improvise by picking another card each day and placing it in between the Fool and the World. This card will highlight where to place your focus, giving you that extra daily guidance to take you closer to your goal.

I like to mix and match with the cards, as I do in my readings. For the middle energy I pick an oracle card for the practical everyday advice I need. At the time of writing, I am using The Clown (Fool) and The Big Medicine Wheel (World) from one of my favourite decks, *The Vision Quest Tarot*, and the middle card is Oak from *The Magic Of Nature Oracle* sitting perfectly between them. Oak is all about discipline, and just what I need to support me at this time. If we are lacking in discipline in life, it literally drains us of energy. So, as daily guidance to stay on track with your goals, it's good advice.

IN A NUTSHELL

As a vehicle for your abundance journey, using cards brings heightened creativity and magic to your practice. These workings can easily be used for health or any other area of your life too. The more specific you are in your intentions, the more precise the guidance will be.

The tools of the Witch are the tools of a Magician... and honing your skills of divination will serve you well in creating a magical life. I must admit, as a teacher and reader of the tarot, the cards are one of my favourite magical tools. Working with symbolism in the form of beautiful imagery – and let's face it, there are so many beautiful decks to choose from nowadays – is an absolute pleasure for me.

You can benefit from the tarot in so many ways. It's beyond the scope of this book to go into more detail, but do learn as much as you can, and you will find that they will become a wise friend, as they have to me. I have listed some useful books and some of my favourite working decks in the *Further Reading* section at the back of the book.

Now, are you ready to find out what a master magician can teach you? Let's move on to the next chapter and meet him.

8
MEETING AMERGIN

*We are what we imagine ourselves to be –
Dolores Ashcroft-Nowicki*

Becoming rich in thought, feeling and action will align you with the magic of abundance. To go further, we must imagine further. We must look far beyond our current bounds in order to create fabulous wealth in our lives. This is only possible when we practise conscious, focused and unfettered dreaming.

It's good to aim high, but not if you can't see your target. It's good to dream big, but imagination is a muscle, and like any muscle, it needs to be worked to make it strong. How, as magical practitioners, do we work our dreaming muscle?

Amergin

Amergin is a poet and magician from Irish mythology. He won Ireland for the Gaelic people by speaking a poem-spell in which he identified himself with the wind, sea, the wild boar and the salmon. By saying 'I am the wind', and knowing it to be true, he became one with the wind and channelled its power.

Try saying 'I am the wind'. Probably nothing will happen. Amergin's words were not just words, but a spell. This is because of the *focus* with which he spoke them, and because of his capacity to dream far out beyond himself. His strength of focus and strength of dreaming allowed him to identify with things as vast and elemental as the wind and the waves.

His focused attention was like an arrowhead or the point of a sword: deadly sharp, not dulled by distraction or by dreaming small.

Can you be like Amergin, concentrating your entire attention on a single point of desire?

Can you banish all distractions in order to maximise your chances of success?

Can you become the point of a sword?

WITCH WAYS

Here is your chance to meet this great magician and receive some guidance.

A Pathworking with Amergin

Listen to the audio version here: **bit.ly/3piXA5e**

Begin your connection to your magical self with **solitude** and **stillness**.

- Take a few deep breaths and relax.

- Imagine putting down roots of golden light into the earth, travelling deeper into the ground with every breath. You take in the earth's energy. Feel it glowing and flowing around your body, its golden light warming and filling every cell... and you let it flow out through the soles of your feet, like roots spreading back into the earth.

- Take no notice of your thoughts; let them come and go like passing traffic.

- Engage all your senses, and remember that what you see and hear and what you smell and feel will add power to your experience... building the images around you as you go.

- Feel the energy flow increasing as you open your mind and shift your focus from the outside world to the inner planes and your third eye centre.

Visualise a doorway leading out of the room. Open it and walk through it, closing it behind you.

You find yourself shrouded in a heavy mist, and look down to see a path just visible at your feet. You begin to follow it slowly, feeling the mist lightly touching your skin. It's comforting. *All is well,* it seems to be saying. *Follow me.*

Taking your time, you make your way along the path where the mist eventually clears to reveal a cloudy sky and a coastline below. Here, a sandy beach stretches out to a sea of white rolling waves tumbling onto large craggy stones.

The wind picks up, and you follow the path down to the beach and look out to the ocean, where a ship becomes visible amongst the rolling waves. And there on the prow of the ship is a tall man, long hair blowing in the wind, in a bright emerald cloak shimmering under the darkening sky.

For a moment, the figure disappears, and all you can see are the waves rolling in faster with the wind, crashing onto the shoreline. There's a stillness in the air and you can hear a voice over the wind.

'I see you, Magical One. I see the fire in your head, the treasure in your heart... the burning desire for knowledge and the calling to serve. You must learn how to bend and sway with the wind, roll in and out with the tides... grow light and dark with the moon, and shine fiercely like the sun. You must do all of these things and more...'

The words fade into the distance.

The wind picks up once again and waves crash louder upon the shore. Suddenly you feel unsteady... the wind and water hit your face, and you look down to see the emerald cloak, dark and wet, clinging to your body.

You are on the prow of the ship looking out to the ocean. The storm rages around you, and you are gripped by a power you can't control. It surges within you and rises up from deep inside, and raising your arms to the heavens you sing out to the ocean:

> *I am the wind on the sea*
> *I am the wave of the sea*
> *I am the bull of seven battles*
> *I am the eagle on the rock*
> *I am a flash from the sun*
> *I am the most beautiful of plants*
> *I am a strong wild boar*
> *I am a salmon in the water*
> *I am a lake in the plain*
> *I am the word of knowledge*
> *I am the head of the spear in battle*
> *I am the god that puts fire in your head*
> *Who spreads light in the gathering on the hills?*
> *Who can tell the ages of the moon?*
> *Who can tell the place where the sun rests?*
> *It is I.*

As you speak of water, boar and spear, your mind reaches out and becomes one with them all. The power of eagle and bull, fire and wave, spear and setting sun fill your body. You can actually feel yourself channelling the life force of these beings and reaching out across all of creation.

And then, the sea becomes still, the waves flatten and the wind drops. An oystercatcher calls out, echoing across the water... The spell has silenced the storm.

You are no longer on the ship, but look down to feel sand between your toes and the sun on your face, but it doesn't bother you. *Nothing* distracts you.

In fact, you've never felt more certain about who you are... and why you're here in this moment. You feel it in your blood and bones. Your body pulses with the wildness of the elements, and your mind buzzes with familiar words playing on your tongue as you speak them out loud to the land, sea and sky:

> *I am the point of a sword filled*
> *with the power of every being,*
> *to silence the storm.*

This is who you are. This is what you've become. You are Amergin and *he* is you. Ponder on this for a while...

PAUSE FOR A FEW MINUTES

Gradually, you come back from your dreamtime and notice you are once again dressed as you were before. But you are not the same. You will *never* be the same again.

The dark clouds have shifted to blue skies, and the sun lingers on your skin. You return to the path and walk back through the mist until you reach the door once again.

- You walk through the door and back into the room.

- Take a deep breath in and feel yourself back in the physical body. Take another deep breath in and feel yourself back in the physical body. You are fully grounded.

- Wriggle your fingers and toes, stretch gently, and when you're ready... open your eyes.

Welcome back.
THE MAGIC IS DONE.

After spending time with Amergin, how are you feeling? Write down your experience and what it means to you.

IN A NUTSHELL

The Witch is a spell weaver. We learn how to focus with such intent that the point of our focus resembles the point of a sword.

Do you have the magical imagination to look beyond the storm? Can you weave a spell to create the changes you seek? How about dedicating and devoting yourself to the task at hand with such intensity that distractions fade from your awareness?

When you become so focused on one thing it cancels out anything that dares to draw you away from it.

Like Amergin, when you become the point of a sword, *nothing* can stand in your way.

9
PROSPER WITH THE MOON

You are prosperous to the degree that you are experiencing peace, health, and plenty in your world – Catherine Ponder

Witches have many tools at their disposal, and working effective magic is about using the most efficient tools to achieve our end goal.

If the end goal is to achieve riches on every level, then we have to understand this is something that is not going to happen overnight. In fact, a vision of that calibre is a long-term goal and so will require long-term thinking, feeling and actions targeted towards it.

It requires *patience*. Are you ready for that? If you are, I assure you it will be worth it.

Working with the moon's energy adds power to our magic over time as she is continually on the move, growing, peaking and decreasing in energy throughout her cycle. The moon will not only teach you patience. She will lead you into the deep mysteries of the hidden realms and show you magic.

Who Is the Moon?

Let's look at some of her magical aspects. It's a good way to get a feel for this amazing silver lady in our skies.

The moon is Lady of the Night and calls us inwards to look beneath the surface of our lives. She takes us into the mystery of life and illuminates the dark crevices in ourselves. She represents the Triple Goddess energy in her guise as Maiden, Mother and Crone; the feminine principle (Yin); and wields her unearthly power over us, stirring our emotions, which can sometimes be confusing and leave us groping around in the dark.

Solutions are found intuitively rather than logically with her guidance as she casts shadows and yet illuminates the secrets of our innermost selves. However, if we align ourselves with the ebb and flow of her cycles and can be still and quiet enough to listen, her wisdom will reach us. When we work with her energy, we embrace the mystery of life and all it can teach us.

Moon Cycles

One of the most magical guides is the moon. By working with her energy we come into closer relationship with our own. And we are fortunate as Witches, that we have the most stunning support in lunar energy around us all the time. By tapping into the moon and her cycles we can align our own energy field to be in harmony with our dreams and visions of the future while staying present with the deep magic of the moment.

Lunar energy has long been used to aid and support magical practices and spellwork of all kinds. Our ancestors learned to navigate their lives in many ways with the moon as a compass. From an agricultural perspective, they would plant the precious seeds of their future crops at the most fertile times and found that certain moon phases supported their purposes.

The Witch tunes into the natural cycles, seasons and tides of energy to support whatever they're working on in life. Aligning with a particular moon phase adds power to your practice. And it's the practice of the craft that hones your skills and develops your abilities. Every time you create a working based on magical attunement you raise the power *within yourself*. The magic is inside you, and the change always begins there.

How long does the moon cycle last for?

The moon is subject to more than one cycle, but the basics are the moon phases, or *faces* as I like to think of them. The moon face cycle lasts for twenty-nine and a half days. These follow the cycle of new... waxing... full... waning... dark... new... and so it continues.

Remember to correspond your magic with each phase: Work for increase, drawing energy towards you, as she grows and peaks... and work for decrease, releasing energy, as she grows smaller.

WITCH WAYS
New Moon – The Maiden

The new moon is a time of rebirth and hope and lasts for three and a half days. It's a great time for setting intentions and making plans. The beginning of a new project or venture will benefit from this creative lunar energy at the start of her cycle. Apply for that job, start the diet or open a savings account. Begin again with anything that hasn't quite worked out before... kick a bad habit and start a good one.

Remember that your intention determines the *direction* you will move in, and the goals you set yourself will arise naturally from that. These will then become the way you measure your progress, one step at a time. This is why it's a great time for working magic with the wind spirits as the element of Air is associated with the power of the mind: our thoughts and ideas. If you intend to live a life of happiness, health, wisdom and wealth, this makes up the recipe for riches in your life.

A Witch's Ladder of Prosperity

Feathers are the perfect ingredient for this spell.

YOU WILL NEED:
- Four feathers that have been gifted to you by different birds
- A strong piece of cord about 45 cm/18 inches in length
- A hag stone

WHAT TO DO:
- On a new moon, tune into your intentions for the coming lunar cycle.
- As you tie each feather to the cord, think about what it means in your life.
- For the first feather, focus on Happiness.
- For the second feather, focus on Health.
- For the third feather, focus on Wisdom.
- For the fourth feather, focus on Wealth.
- Knot the hag stone at the bottom and seal your intention with these words:

I grow richer every day
Prospering in every way
Mother, Maiden, Crone are
one
As I will and harm to none

- Hang your Witch ladder outside on a tree in your garden or backyard.
- Return the feathers to Mother Earth as the magic manifests in your life.

Waxing Moon

The waxing moon has two phases. Between three and a half and seven days after the new moon, is the waxing crescent, and the waxing gibbous appears between ten and a half and fourteen days after the new moon. In general, when the moon is waxing, it's a good time to act on what you want to increase in your life. Use it as a time to grow your communications, opportunities, and your income.

In the run-up to the full moon, tap into the energy of increase in this cycle to motivate you in the direction of your magical intent. Those new projects or goals you began at the new moon can move up a gear now, and tuning into the increasing opportunities will push you to forge ahead and maximise your full potential.

It's all about growth.

And remember, when you are growing, you are connected to an abundant source of positive and vibrant energy.

Magic for Promotion

There are many ways of using the energy of a waxing moon to increase your income. But remember to be open to the opportunities that present themselves to earn rather than expecting a windfall. I'm not discounting that could occur, but don't rely on it.

Here's a very simple spell that will certainly help to open you up to all the avenues in which you can receive money.

YOU WILL NEED:
- A green candle – but if you don't have a green candle, use any colour and make sure your intent is clear.
- A pocket knife or a nail file
- Eight coins
- The Eight of Pentacles tarot card
- A hag stone

WHAT TO DO:
On a waxing crescent moon gather your tools, set up your sacred space, and spend time contemplating your intention. I like to say or sing a chant as a way of doing this. The voice is an instrument... and you will be adding power to your magic through the vibration of sound.

Here is a chant I use to help me work with this energy:

> *The more I learn the way is clearer*
> *The more I earn is getting nearer*
> *The more I learn, the more I earn...*

I love to work with rhythm and rhyme; it's the poet and songwriter in me. But you can also create your own chants. Think about a word that reflects your intention and play around with it in your mind and on your tongue. And before you know it, another word will appear to rhyme with it. Try it!

I've used *learn* and *earn* in this chant. By focusing on the idea of increase and getting in the flow of that feeling, the words start to form in your mind, and before you know it, you're singing them!

Continuing with the spell...

- Once you have your chant worked out, or have decided

to use mine, carve a pentacle or a money symbol on the side of the candle.

- Light the candle.

- Take your tarot card and prop it up on your altar with the coins around it.

- Hold your hag stone and chant for a good five minutes, the longer the better.

Alternatively, you can go out on a Witch Walk and chant in rhythm with your steps. Put in a twirl here and there, and dance like nobody's watching... I often do! Put your heart and soul into your Witch work and the magic will flow.

Full Moon – The Mother

The moon as the mother is the bringer of all things to fruition. She is the fullness of being, giving birth to creation, and a great time for manifesting abundance, love and creativity. This is also an excellent time to plug into that high energy and charge up your Witch power and your tools in the full moonlight.

However, some of us can feel wired and our energy scattered at this time as we sense the pull of the sun and the moon in opposite directions. You may have trouble sleeping and become especially creative when the moon is full. I know Witches who are deeply inspired and write and paint like crazy into the early hours as she grows to full power.

I'm one of them, and you may be too.

Tides and Beaches

Because the moon governs the tides of the planet, when she is full the ocean tides can be extreme, and if you live on the coastline, you will experience this. As I live by the sea and visit the beach daily with my dogs, my favourite time is at full moon when the magic of nature is abundant and often wild.

Drawing down the moon is a wonderful way to feel her magic and put it to good use with a spell of some kind. In the summer I love to gather with others and celebrate with a fire, music and storytelling, and watch the moon come up over the water. There are few things quite as magical as that sight.

Nuclear versus Lunar

In our small coastal village we have a nuclear power station that is in the process of being decommissioned. A few years ago, there was talk about the Chinese government building a new station in place of the old one. At the time my husband Ian and I joined some local protesters in boats out on the water, and afterwards I organised a gathering on the beach in front of the old station. I wanted to do something to protect the land and the environment, so we performed a healing ceremony at full moon.

Warrior Queens

We called in the battle goddesses, and in came the Morrigan, Maeve, Scáthach and Andraste, four of the most powerful warrior queens, to support us in our ritual. We donned war paint, drummed, chanted, and cast our intentions out under that beautiful full moon, drawing down her energy as we called in the divine feminine in her fiercest of guises to protect the land and the sea. Magically, we did all we could to put the guardianship of the environment in place.

It was an evening I will never forget. Filled with inspiration afterwards, I wrote a song that remains close to my heart, as it reminds me of the power we tuned into that night on the beach.

Magical Music

'Draw Her Down' is one of my favourite Morrigans Path songs, and whenever I hear it, I'm taken back to that magical night. Have a listen to it, and if there is anything you are battling with at the moment by all means use it for protection.

Listen to the audio version of the song here: **bit.ly/3Pu9R1n**
Music can be one of the most potent forms of magic, especially when it's drawn from the power of a full moon, and created with a specific intent.

There is no greater tool than natural sources of energy… and with nature at your fingertips, you have access to magic whenever you need it. Tap into that power on a full moon, draw her down, and use it to strengthen and focus your work. Use it to amplify your power and sing your intentions to the Gods. They will hear you.

Draw Her Down

- Visit a beach or a natural body of water on a full moon.

- Take plenty of warm clothing, wood for a fire, musical instruments and friends!

- Make sure it's safe and legal to light a fire and set up camp for the evening.

- Make offerings to the fire and the moon goddess of kindling and dried bunches of herbs… with prayers and healing thoughts, spoken or sung.

- Watch the moon rise with singing, chanting and dancing to celebrate.

- Divine with cards, runes, bones, shells, feathers or flames.

ALTERNATIVELY
You can go outside on your own:
* Stand under the moon, raise your arms to the sky, and invite her energy into you by singing this chant:

Lady of the moon, sing your tune through me
Lady of the moon, dance and set me free

Whether you draw her down with others or by yourself, you will be fully charged to power up your magic with the riches of the lunar goddess.

Waning Moon - The Crone

As in the phase of the waxing moon, the waning moon phase lasts for approximately half the time of the whole cycle, with the waning gibbous appearing three and a half days to seven days after the full moon. In the waning crescent phase, she appears between ten and a half days after the full moon and up until the new moon.

The waning moon is a good time for banishing. As the moon decreases in size, the Crone Goddess calls us to release anything which has outgrown its space or time in our lives. Any negative emotions you may be holding onto, exhaustion caused by excess (burnout), or addictive behaviour can all be dealt with at this time.

Banish with the waning moon any weakness of character, such as emotional cowardice or un-forgiveness, and all feelings of isolation and fear of change. You can get rid of a lot of unwanted obstacles and blockages in your energy field with this moon phase. She's very handy!

As you tune into the power of decreasing energy, you may feel a natural urge to slow down. The Crone is a fantastic spirit guide if you're fearful or worried about anything, as she will bring in the wisdom of experience to light your way in the dark.

Work this spell to break free from all restrictions and trappings of any kind.

Breaking Chains of Negativity

You will need:

- The Devil tarot card or a picture of the devil you have drawn yourself
- A hag stone to represent the Crone
- A dark-coloured candle
- A necklace chain

What to do:

- On a waning moon place the chain (with the clasp fastened) in a circle on your altar and prop the Devil up behind it.
- Light the candle and take the hag stone and hold it lightly in both hands.
- Contemplate all the things in your life that are burdensome, that no longer have a purpose in your life. These are the chains that bind you. What situations, relationships or habits are weighing you down?
- Give them all to the hag stone. Imbue it with everything you can think of that is holding you back from your true creative path. What can you give to the

Crone?

- Undo the clasp of the chain and stretch it out on the altar. Keep hold of the hag stone, place it over your heart and listen.

- Take your time with this practice; be passive and open and trust the answers will come.

- Slowly say to yourself: *I release all that holds me back*

- See all the things that weigh you down fading, and feel the energy shifting...

- Keep your focus on your heart and call in the Crone.

- Be open to any impressions you receive in your mind or body, no matter how subtle... and observe.

Keep asking the Crone to help, and she will. It may not come straight away, but later when you have completely forgotten about it. Out of the blue you may feel the urge to do something or contact someone. It will feel like guidance. Acknowledge it and act upon it as long as it feels right.

Be patient and give yourself plenty of time with this practice.

Dark Moon – The Crone

The dark moon is any time over the three days before the new moon when the sky is dark. It's a time of stillness and finding comfort in the darkness. We are called to retreat and spend time in the cave with the Crone Goddess. This is a good time to pause, to rest and reflect, and work on ending any cycles of lack.

We are often faced with the shadow of ourselves at the dark moon, and weariness may call us to slow down and rest. We can use this time to withdraw and contemplate what prevents us from taking the actions needed to create and live a prosperous life. This action alone will help to clear our energy field and calm our nervous system.

Making incense for a particular purpose is a very effective way of working magic. I find that thinking about what I need, and then looking up the ingredients and spending the time contemplating the reasons for my purpose is an act of deep immersion into the energy of it. It puts me into the right feeling state, and for the magic to be potent, that is what we need to do: feel our way through it. The more we can engage our feelings with the work, the more powerful it will be.

So how can the dark moon phase help us create a magical life of abundance?

Try this spell.

Ending Lack

You will need:

- Dried rosemary and vervain

- Dried tulip petals

- Dragon's blood resin and sea salt

- Charcoal for burning

- Mortar and pestle

- Cauldron

- A green garnet stone – grossular or uvarovite (excellent for healing the feeling of scarcity in all its aspects:

finances, self-confidence, love, power and knowledge)
- The World tarot card
- Coloured crayons or pens
- A square piece of paper
- Tea light

WHAT TO DO:

At the time of the dark moon, retreat to your sacred space and make sure you will be undisturbed (no people, phones or digital devices). Gather your ingredients for the incense and mix together with your mortar and pestle. Light the charcoal in your cauldron, set aside the incense, and make yourself comfortable while holding the green garnet in your left hand.

Meeting the Ogre of Lack

Focus on your connection to the invisible realms with **stillness, silence** and **solitude**.

Close your eyes and use the breath to relax your body completely, inhaling positive energy and feeling it absorb and filter through every layer of your being. Exhale and watch this positive energy as it becomes a golden glow around you. Feel its warmth and protection holding you, bask in the light as it radiates around you and through you relaxing every muscle and cell in your body. All is good.

Diving into the Well of You

- You are standing at the edge of a deep well, and looking down into the water, you feel it pull you down…

- As you go deeper into the well, you know that you are seeking out the place where poverty lives. Where is it?

- As you spiral down into the darkness, you hear the faint echo of footsteps getting closer.

- You can hear a voice calling your name. What does it sound like?

- And now you can see the shape of a figure forming in front of you. What does it look like?

- Allow it to come as close as you can handle…

- Now ask the being, *What is your purpose?* Be patient and listen for the answer.

- Now ask it, *What do you want?* and *Why do you stay here?*

- When you have received your answers, tell the ogre you no longer need him. Thank him for coming and bid him farewell.

- See the figure becoming smaller and hear the fading footsteps as it walks away.

- Begin to spiral back up through the depths of the well, feeling the water carrying you… and the light from above drawing you back to the top.

- Take some deep breaths and feel your feet on the ground and the good earth beneath you.

- Now take the paper and the crayons/pens and draw the image of what you saw in the well. Remember what it said to you and draw anything you can remember, whatever comes to mind: words or images… it doesn't matter.

- How do you feel about it? Draw that. The idea is to get it out and onto the paper.

- When you have finished, sprinkle the incense into the centre of the paper and add the salt.

- Twist the bundle until it's closed and place it on top of the burning (white) charcoal.

- Watch the herbs smoulder and see all the poverty and lack in your life leaving... disappearing. Know that you have cut off the supply of this energy and it has gone.

- How does that feel? Explore and enjoy the feeling.

- Burn the remains of the paper and bury the ashes in the earth.

- Carry the green garnet or place it on your altar for one lunar cycle.

THE MAGIC IS DONE.

Riches for Witches

Planting an acorn on a dark moon is a great way to boost your work to end any cycles of lack. It's a way to ensure that you will experience prosperity and abundance in the present moment: your place of power.

As you plant your acorn, sing this spell to the earth and know that she hears you. Imagine what you are singing about, feel it and know it is already happening *right now*.

> *In the darkness I am growing, I am growing, I am growing...*

> *I am seeing riches flowing, riches flowing, riches flowing!*
> *Power of oak and lunar tide*
> *Ending lack I open wide*
> *Now abundance I am seeing, I am seeing, I am seeing...*
> *Is the magic I am being, I am being, I am being!*
> *Power of oak and lunar tide*
> *Ending lack I open wide*
> *To the earth and all her riches, all her riches, all her riches...*
> *Hear the wisdom of the witches, of the witches, of the witches!*
> *Power of oak and lunar tide*
> *Ending lack I open wide*
> *In the darkness I am growing...(ad lib)*

Build the energy by repeating the chant as many times as you like. This a great way of working magic with others. Everyone brings an acorn to the gathering with a pot of compost and sings the spell together as they plant the acorn.

Singing and dancing are two of the most powerful ways to raise energy and send your intentions out into the cosmos.

It's how we amplify our magic.

In a Nutshell

Working with the moon will enrich your life on all levels as you discover the extent of her potential, and experience your own, with each moon phase. When you align yourself with the lunar cycle you will empower your magic to ebb and flow with her magical tides.

Remember to work from new moon to full moon for growing and increasing prosperity, and from waning moon to dark moon for releasing anything that stands in your way of being prosperous.

Whatever the moon phase is as you're reading this, is a good time for you to work with her. There is always something she can offer that you will prosper from.

Now you can send out your intentions and cast your spells with growing confidence in your ability to create riches and change your life for the better.

DIGGING FOR GOLD

10
GOING DEEPER

Get down, deeper and down – Status Quo

Now you have dreamed of the abundance you seek, it's time for the spade work. Let's dig in deep and focus on our inner Air nature. It's a powerful tool for moving forward. Air is the magic of our mind and the process of inspiration. It's the mental energy of transmitting and expanding our thoughts and ideas through speech and communication as well as the physical breath.

It's the power of discipline and patience, used in divination and meditation. These tools and techniques will support us and provide a structure for our work, fine-tuning our abundance vibration. They will help us in our efforts to grow and become richer.

Clearing the Debris

We have to work in earnest now to remove from our energy field, *everything* that limits our abundance, which is all the beliefs and thought patterns of lack lurking in the shadow self.

And of course, it helps to know what these things are so that we can work on excavating the dirt lying in our way. But like any miner who works in the dark, we need a light to show us the way.

How else can we expect to find our gold?

The Witch works with the light of magical awareness. Do not underestimate your light. It's the most powerful tool you have. All of your spadework in magical development involves honing the skills that help you to see and to know. Every tool that brings all that is hidden to the surface of your consciousness, will shine the light of your awareness brighter.

Divination and Seership

One of the most effective tools we have for digging down is the art of divination. Asking the Gods is one of the oldest and most ancient forms of seership: making the unknown known. Many Witches are naturally tuned in to this wavelength. You may already be on it yourself. You seem to know things about people, places or situations and are able to see what is going to happen. What isn't always obvious to others has always appeared obvious and quite natural to you. Sound familiar?

You may have your own way of divining, through dreams or reading signs in nature: in the shape of clouds, the flight of animals, or other means of discernment to determine guidance from the wisdom of the spirit world. The Druid ovates, known as *ofyddion* in Iron Age Celtic Britain, were the professional diviners and seers, whereas in Ireland they were called *faithi*.

Rulers have also been known to use divination, as did the warrior queen of the Iceni, Boudicca. Before battle, she made an augury of releasing a hare from the folds of her robes and watched its track. As the hare was the symbol of the Goddess, the direction it ran in was seen to be victorious, and Boudicca went on to lead her people to victory against the Romans.

Oracles

Oracle is 'to speak' – to pass on knowledge built on the wisdom of the past. An oracle does not necessarily predict future events but directs our attention to choices in the present moment which can influence the future. Our power lies in the *now*, and recognising this enables us to become truly responsible for everything we think, feel and do.

The Witch is a practical being. Wisdom is earned through experience and in the practice of the craft. Magic does not just happen. Divine timing is magical timing. Our tools tune us into the witch wavelength. They act as a compass for our energy, guiding us creatively to see and know what to do in any given situation.

Oracles are the bridge between this world and the next. They work through the language of symbols, and the Witch speaks the language well. It's a magical language, alive with ancient wisdom and creative potential. The oracles we use are a means of communication and speak to our souls, which is why some will resonate with you while others won't.

The tarot has always spoken to me, but the ogham never has, although I would love to learn more about it. I love the runes but the I-Ching befuddles my brain completely.

When your soul recognises certain symbols in an oracle, it will speak a language that feels familiar. The oracle will talk to you. Let it speak, and learn by playing with a tool to get to know it.

SOME EXAMPLES:

- Cards – tarot & other themed oracle decks e.g. angel, faeries, nature, ascended masters, etc.
- Runes, bones and stones
- Numerology and astrology
- Dowsing – pendulum, hazel rods,
- Ogham – Celtic tree alphabet

- I-Ching – ancient Chinese oracle

- Ouija board

- Scrying – crystal ball, tea leaves, fire, water, clouds, entrails, etc.

- Celtic shaman's tools – drum, crane bag, rattles, flutes and whistles

These are just some of the many divination tools to seek knowledge, guidance and inspiration from the Otherworld.

You will no doubt have a few shop-bought treasures, but if you can find your own tools naturally out on the land, they will bring the magic of the earth to your witchery in all kinds of ways. I have a beautiful set of runes that took me months of Witch Walking on the beach to find. But eventually, I had a set of sandstones worn smooth by the sea and they are all the more valuable to me because of it.

Hag stones, shells, feathers and driftwood all find their way back from the beach with me, and the elements speak through every one of them. The magic of nature is an oracle and the earth offers it to us freely.

Go out on the land and make time for your magic. Tune into it, and it will seek you out.

The Art of Patience

When we have clarity on a particular issue or problem, we can do something about it. We can work with the energy to light up those dark areas and gradually make progress. And it *is* a gradual process, so the first thing we must focus on developing an abundant supply of is *patience*.

Patience pays off as you build trust in the idea that the wait will be worthwhile. I can tell you that it will be totally worth it if you are willing to do the work and take your time with the process.

What's the Hurry?

You may feel that you want to move forwards more quickly than life is allowing you to at the moment. Before you let frustration get the better of you, try and see the benefits of extra time. This is why being patient with *yourself* is one of the best self-care tools you have in your toolbox. Give your inner Witch time to digest what you're learning before moving on to the next step.

Waking up to your Witch power is an ongoing process best taken slowly. Patience will save you time and frustration, and persistence is your friend. Repeat the practices you do until you begin to feel the shifts in your consciousness. Valuing your time is valuing yourself.

There are no shortcuts on the road to riches and no bypasses on the spiritual path. Your time is precious and there is plenty of it. Use it wisely and trust in divine timing.

Meditation

A regular meditation practice is important to balance and steady the mind. Mental health is something that can be easily taken for granted but can never be ignored. Meditation forms the basis of your Witch work and is crucial to psychic development. There are many benefits.

Meditating daily helps to:
- Improve concentration, memory and creative thinking
- Reduce stress
- Decrease blood pressure

- Enhance ability to sleep
- Reduce chronic pain
- Improve emotional and mental health
- Enhance self-understanding and support spiritual development

Meditation will also help you to experience your sense of the non-physical. By detaching from the senses of sight, sound, feeling, taste and touch, what are you left with? Your thoughts. By disengaging and becoming the witness of your thoughts you will still the mental chatter to a point where you don't notice it as much if at all.

With practice, your mind will quieten and you will be able to hold an image in your mind without becoming attached to your thoughts.

A SIMPLE MEDITATION PRACTICE:

- Create undisturbed time for this daily practice on a regular basis.
- Unplug from digital devices.
- Light a candle and some incense, and put on some relaxing music if it helps. None of these are necessities but will help to create a calm environment. Set a timer for five minutes.
- Sit comfortably in a chair with your spine straight and your feet on the floor.
- Focus on relaxing your body by becoming aware of any tension and letting it drain into the earth.

- Close your eyes and inhale deeply... exhaling slowly.

- Continue to follow the breath and focus your mind on one thing. If your mind is busy, try staring at the candle flame and repeating a simple mantra in your head... *I am calm.*

- As soon as your mind jumps in with a thought, acknowledge it and return to your breath and the mantra. You are training your mind to concentrate.

- Try this every day, slowly building up to ten minutes, then twenty, then half an hour.

If you want to develop your psychic faculty, improve your ability to focus, and expand your mind, a daily meditation practice is non-negotiable. My own meditation practice tends to be a part of my yoga practice which I do as much as possible, but it's not always every day. However, before I write, which is daily, I will sit at my desk, light a candle and sit in stillness and silence for about five or ten minutes. This really helps to clear my mind and set me up for the work ahead. Sometimes I struggle with resistance; the mind is an insidious beast. But I do it anyway.

What's important is that we make time for it, however long or short it is. Even as you wait for the kettle to boil, at a traffic light or in a queue somewhere, taking time to be at peace with yourself in silence and stillness is time well spent. How many of us mindlessly scroll through our phones at any given opportunity? I've done it, still do it and I'm pretty sure you do it too!

Meditation has never been more greatly needed than now in the modern world. The digital age is not only around us; it's inside our heads. It has burrowed into our brains and feeds on our attention, whether we are conscious of it or not.

What do we do with this digital parasite?

Detoxify

How much time are you spending online? Whatever you're spending time doing, whether it's shopping, social media, or staring at apps on your phone you can easily find yourself consuming for most of that time.

Halfway to solving a problem is being aware of it. If you are feeling overwhelmed with too much going on in your head, can't think straight, and are getting anxious over the slightest thing, it's time for a digital detox. Excessive consumption of anything will not do you any good at all.

When I started writing in a different genre a couple of years ago, I wanted to free up some headspace for the story, as there was a lot of planning to do. So I stopped using social media for about four months, and it was liberating on every level. Without the distraction, I could focus deeply on what I had to do without anyone else's thoughts or comments in my head.

Needless to say, it didn't last, but it was a great lesson! We can change anything we really want to when our desire and motivation are strong enough to make those changes.

Discipline

Having the discipline to detach and detoxify from what is not doing us any good is a skill we can learn. But it starts with awareness. Once you know and understand this, you can remedy it. You can do something about it. It might be a relationship that's driving you nuts, or a situation or a job that dulls your senses... it could be both!

Once you know what it is, and have decided what you are going to do about it, don't waste any time. ACT. Remove yourself from the problem or remove it from you. Put down your phone, end the relationship, leave the job. You get the picture.

Witch Ways
Connection

Stop over-consuming and start creating.

Give yourself a break, and some breathing space. Create time daily when the calmness of your thoughts is a priority, and you become a clear channel for your highest good. You do it by strengthening your connection to your magical self.

There are a number of ways you can go about this.

Through stillness and solitude

- Static meditation
- Prayer
- Pathworking – listening to a guided narrative

Through movement

- Witch Walking
- Dancing
- Yoga
- Tai Chi

Through the voice

- Singing
- Chanting

Through art

- Writing
- Painting
- Crafts

When we allow ourselves time away from the seduction of consumerism, we move into a space of unlimited creative potential.

A Witch Walk to Lighten Up

After focusing on our Air nature, it's time to ground the work with Earth and Water on a Witch Walk. This is a powerful releasing practice you can do by yourself or with a friend.
    Use it for your Witch Walk and enjoy.

You will need:

- A small backpack to carry on your shoulders
- A pack of four to six small bottles of water
- A permanent marker pen

What to do:

- Spend some time contemplating what is holding you back in these areas of your life:
Bad habits
Loss or trauma from the past

Procrastination in the present
Fear and anxiety about the future
Unforgiveness
Relationships

- Write down your burdens under these headings on each bottle.

For example:
Bad habits – *what pattern of thinking or behaviour is not doing you any good?*
Loss – *what past trauma are you suppressing or holding onto?*
Procrastination – *what are you putting off?*
Fears – *what are you worrying about that hasn't happened?*
Unforgiveness – *what are you feeling guilty about or blaming yourself or someone else for?*
Relationships – *who have you outgrown?*

- Choose a time and a place to go for a walk. A rural setting is ideal, or a park if you live in an urban area.

- Fill your backpack with the bottles of water and put it on.

- Begin your walk by setting your intention to let go of all that is weighing you down and holding you back from your abundance.

- Walk for as long as you can while contemplating all the things in your life that you are holding onto.

- Stop when you feel tired and take out one of the bottles of water. Thinking about what you are releasing, pour out the water somewhere safe and appropriate – into the ground or down a drain.
Say to yourself or chant out loud:
Castaway and be gone, I give it away to the earth and she makes me strong.

- Put the empty bottle in a bin or in your backpack.

- Continue walking, stopping to repeat the process while chanting, until every bottle has been emptied.

- Carry on walking with your lighter backpack and notice how you feel.

- Finish your walk by lighting a ritual candle upon your return home to thank Mother Earth for holding and healing you.

THE MAGIC IS DONE.

Every element has been involved in this practice. You have chanted with Air, released with Water, walked with Earth, and ritualised with Fire, while Spirit binds every element to empower your intentions.

Physically releasing the weight of mental and emotional burdens can have a profound effect on you as you experience the power of lightening up on every level. Discuss your experience and share it with your companions. Record it in your magical journal and repeat it whenever you feel the need.

In a Nutshell

Whether you go through the process in solitude or in the company of others, when you dig deep into yourself and remove the debris in your energy field, you create space to grow. Divination and working with oracles is a great magical tool for this purpose, allowing anything that blocks your abundance to rise to the surface and be removed.

Working with stillness, movement, the voice and art all help to strengthen your connection with your magical nature, your direct line to Spirit.

And while Witch Walking is not only a liberating practice all-round, it also helps you in becoming a clear and open channel for divine guidance.

Are you ready to go further, Magical One? It's time to plunge into darkness.

11
DARK RICHES

There is a crack in everything, that's how the light gets in – Leonard Cohen

Who turned the lights out? Time to move over to the dark side for a while. You can handle it, I know it. But make sure you bring your sense of humour with you; it's your protection when life gets too serious.

The Dark Side

The good news is your shadow isn't all bad. In fact, I have come to learn over time that mine is a damn good teacher and you will too if you can face up to it and not let it overpower you. That's the key.

I was plunged into darkness when I hit the hormonal hell of mid-life, otherwise known as the men-o-whats-it disease. I can't even bring myself to say the word it's better known for, so I made my own up… it felt much better. You'll find it in *The Madness and the Magic,* my Witch Lit fiction series about Minerva, a crazy menopausal Witch and her ridiculous antics to snare the local (guitar-playing) vicar.

There I was, hexed by the Gods, for no apparent reason other than my age and gender. So I pinned it all on Minerva…

– She was one of those who found themselves teetering on the edge of a life raft reduced to a single plank, worn down by the raging and treacherous currents of an unpredictable and undulating sea of wretched emotions –

If you haven't experienced that or anything like it, because, for one reason or another, you have been blessed by the Gods, count yourself lucky. I don't believe in luck but am quite happy to make an exception to the rule here. And when it comes to the female gender and hormones, I think we can all agree on some level... whether you've encountered them first-hand or second, they are not the easiest or the holiest of things to contend with. How I didn't end up in a divorce court, a padded cell, or behind bars I'll never know. Darkness prevailed on every level.

What Can the Darkness Teach Us?

One of the many gifts of the dark is transformation. The passing of one state of being into another, whether it's a life or a season; it's energy that changes us. In many cultures and spiritual traditions, it is seen as the cycle of death and rebirth, and the journey through the darkness is an initiation into the power of our own self. Balancing the dark and light within us integrates the spiritual and the human being so that we can weave these aspects of our own being into wholeness. For the Witch, it's an act of magic.

Think about the seasons in nature. The darkness is just as much a part of those cycles as the light is. In the wild, nothing in nature blooms all year round, and most living things die back in the winter months. It's a time to slow down, rest and recuperate. And with the dying back of old energy, there is a natural urge to pause and build up the new.

Darkness is a necessary contrast. Night follows day. Imagine if it was daytime all the time... we'd never get to experience the natural beauty of a sunrise or a sunset. And imagine if night-time was a constant. Now that's all right if you're a mushroom, but not much fun for us humans.

Forget about things that go bump in the night. The dark can be a comfort, especially at times of deep introspection.

Endings

The natural passing of one thing to another teaches us to accept what is. Without acceptance, we remain stuck in our thinking and feelings, and resistance to life brings struggle. Death and the pain of grief are prime examples of this. The cycle of life has ended and passes on... the spiritual being experiences human life and then changes back into spirit.

Experiencing the huge tidal waves of grief (as I'm sure you have) once too often in my life, I found the darkness all-consuming. I will not elaborate on that as it belongs in another book, but needless to say, I have also found riches in those times. They have been deeply spiritual times, when, taken to the edge of my world, and glimpsing the other side through the lens of the grim reaper, they taught me something.

The pain of unresolved grief, and fear of the unknown are two major causes of the darkness within us. They are perfectly natural feelings and emotions. And yet as one phase of life passes to another, nothing ever really dies as the circle of life continues. And so the darkness is a time of great alchemy when the opportunity to grow is there for us if we can trust in the process. If we can accept what's going on and move through it with whatever grace we can conjure up for ourselves, the journey through the dark becomes easier. Eventually.

However, if someone had spouted spiritual platitudes to me as I was grieving for the death of my teenage brother, my parents, or my lost youth in the hellfires of a menopausal attack I'd have pinned them to a wall with a pitchfork. And no matter how much anyone tells us to *trust in the process*, what if we can't? What if life leaves us burnt from those fires of hell? Before you reach for the brandy bottle like Minerva, all is not lost. *You* are not lost.

The Guides and the Gods

This is where your spirit guides can step in to show you the way. The Witch knows the natural world and the spirit world are one. The Otherworld is only a thought away, and as close to us as our next breath.

OUR ALLIES ARE HERE TO HELP US:

- The Spirits of Nature – Weather – Seasons
- The Elements – Earth, Air, Fire and Water
- Moon, Sun and Stars
- The Sidhe (faerie beings)
- The Angels
- The Gods and Goddesses/Deities
- The Ancestors

Let's look at some of these spirits to understand how they can help us in our darker times.

Witch Ways
Your Ancestors

Connecting to a loved one is easier than you think it is. No matter how far away you may feel they are, you can close the gap and feel their presence. And if you are already tuned in to the spirit realms, you will be able to bridge that gap more easily than most.

Try this:

- Create a simple sacred space with a photo of your loved one, a rose quartz crystal or a hag stone, and a tea light.

- Light the candle.

- Close your eyes and place a hand on your heart.

- Focus on your breath, inhaling deeply and slowly… and exhaling fully.

- Now bring your beloved to mind. Remember what they looked like, sounded like, and felt like in their physical form. Re-live the experience of being with them.

- Hold them in your mind and feel them in your heart.

- Be with them for as long as you want to.

Feeling their love and sending yours to a loved one is something you can do naturally. Being in that intimate and loving space is a precious gift. Savour it and remember you can do it anytime, anywhere… on a Witch Walk, in the bathroom or doing household chores. The ancestors are not fussy.

You can also connect to a loved one using any of the elements as a portal:

- **Air** – through the breath; talking, singing or chanting.
- **Fire** – lighting a candle or sitting around a fire.
- **Water** – while taking a bath or shower, or by a natural body of water.
- **Earth** – in the company of a tree or in a park or garden.

Keep it simple and natural, and the magic of nature will always be your guide.

Know that your loved ones are always near. We are *never* alone.

Autumn and Winter

These mighty spirits of nature are here to teach us how to work with the energy of release and rest in the darkness. You will know yourself that when the seasons are changing to the darker part of the year, there is a sense of withdrawal and a need for personal space. This leads us to rest and stillness.

Autumn beckons us to release all the things in our lives that we don't need anymore. This can be a build-up of energy from any aspect of our lives that we have grown out of: It could be a job, a place, a relationship, or a condition, habit or belief that doesn't ring true anymore. On a deeper level, unforgiveness can be one of the biggest stumbling blocks that will keep us stuck in the past.

All of these things drain our energy on some level, and it's only by releasing our grip on them that we free ourselves to be present in our life, enjoy the moment and move on without these unwanted burdens.

Working with the spirit of Autumn can teach us to let go and be free of what holds us back.

It heals and liberates us.

Winter, on the other hand, takes us deeper into the darkness and calls us to rest. The Winter spirit wraps itself around us with short days and long nights, bare branches on bony trees, while the north wind doth blow.

When our energy dies back and tiredness sets in, do we listen to our bodies and take time to rest completely? While putting your feet up for months until spring arrives might seem a bit indulgent, it's still a good idea to align with the energy of the season and take more rest than usual. You need it.

It's important to remember that although nothing looks like it's growing in the winter months, the resting period in nature is necessary for growth in the spring. There may be a lull in the life cycle, but seeds are germinating underground as the earth continues to nurture her environment. If you feel weariness calling you to stop, or perhaps life has stopped *you* for some reason, the following is a good practice to do at any time of year.

A Pathworking With Winter

Listen to the audio version here: **bit.ly/42Yc8oA**

Begin your connection to your magical self with **solitude** and **stillness.**

- Feel your breathing deepening and slowing down as you relax your mind and release the tension in your body. Keep breathing deeply and relax completely.

- Feel your mind settling and calming down, allowing the passing traffic of your thoughts to come and go... watching them go by.

- Your mind chatter is becoming quieter, fading into the distance... passing.

- Stay with the breath as it deepens and feel yourself becoming heavier and pulled by the earth beneath you, going deeper and deeper.

- The pulsing of every heartbeat takes you deeper into the earth… into the dark you go… deeper and deeper.

You are travelling along the roots of a tree as they spread out and down, descending into the earth. It feels warm, and the darkness is comforting, wrapping itself around you like a blanket as you are pulled down deeper. The air is damp but you can breathe easily, and you are getting used to the darkness. It feels like an old friend close by your side, watching over you as you travel downwards into the heart of the earth.

Eventually, everything begins to slow down and you stop… and feel the roots that pulled you to this place have flattened out to an uneven earth floor. Steadying yourself, you look around to see the walls of a cave. The sound of water dripping slowly echoes in the distance, and the flickering of an orange flame leads your gaze to a hollow in the wall. You walk through it and see the figure of an elderly woman hunched over a fire.

Her white hair hangs in braids over bony shoulders, and she pulls a long cloak around her as she tends the fire. She breaks sticks from broken branches in a pile beside her. The musky scent of herbs fills the hollow in plumes of smoke, rising like dragons and circling the hollow.

'Come closer, I don't bite.' She speaks to the fire, in a coarse, crackling voice. 'You have travelled far and you must be weary. Come, sit with me and warm yourself.'

Without thinking, you do as she says. You realise that you *are* tired and your muscles ache. You join the old woman as a cold wind cuts across the hollow and the fire draws you closer.

'Who are you?' you have to ask her.

The bony shoulders bounce softly, and she laughs into the flames, before turning to you, bright-eyed and grinning. 'Who do you think I am, Magical One?'

You shrug your shoulders and shake your head slowly, staring into those bright eyes glittering green in the firelight.

The grin widens, and her voice softens, 'I am Winter.'

'So why am I here?'

She shuffles closer to the fire and holds her hands out to the flames.

'Does spending time in the dark worry you? There is everything here to satisfy your needs: warmth, food, and company if you count me! I will provide you with all you need… and most important of all, a time and place to rest. Away from the hustle and bustle of every day you can settle down into yourself and learn to rest. I am talking about deep rest. The darkness has called you and brought you down here… so you might as well get used to it.'

The calmness of her voice irritates you. 'How long will you hold me here for?'

She laughs again, still facing the fire.

'I am not holding you against your will. You came of your own accord… you loosened your grip on your life and left the past where it belongs, behind you. I called you here, yes, but you came freely. The only struggle you have is the way you feel about it and the conflict within you. The struggle is worth nothing, why resist your good?'

She turns and stares at you. What does she mean?

Suddenly your body feels heavy, as you stretch out on the earthen floor among the herbs and the kindling. The fire warms your tired body, and you can feel yourself giving in to the earth beneath you, and the weariness within.

You can hear the old woman's comforting voice in the background.

'It's time to rest now, Magical One. With me, you can do that easily. With me, you can be yourself. There is no part to play, no mask to put on, and no audience to perform to. You are free of all of those things. You are free to receive all that is good for you. You have everything you need: a place to rest, a time to retreat and be filled anew. Reflection will bring understanding, but it will take time. You have plenty of that, you have an *abundance* of it. There is enough here for many lifetimes; it will not escape you. You have enough, there is always enough time for what you need. Stillness and sleep will restore your weariness, silence will bring you peace, and solitude will empower you.'

As you fall into a deep slumber you feel her strong nurturing arms around you, and her soft whisperings, 'Rest now, Magical One. Rest now...'

Spend some time with Winter.

PAUSE FOR A FEW MINUTES

Gradually, you begin to wake from your slumber, slowly stretching your limbs. Yawning, you look around you and see that you are outside in a meadow, lying beside an old oak tree. The air is warm, and you can hear the sound of birdsong rippling through the grass. You touch a primrose scattered in clusters of lemon around the tree, and you smile at a young woman walking past.

She turns to smile back. 'You've had a nice rest... bet you're feeling better now!'

And without a backward glance, she skips away, laughing and waving. You can hear her laughter fading into the distance as you become aware of your surroundings where you are... here in the room.

- Follow your breath as you draw up the earth's energy with each inhalation and exhale the memory of your experience.

- Refreshed and fully awake, you are becoming aware of your physical body. Refreshed and fully awake now... you are becoming aware of your physical body.

- Wriggling your fingers and toes, stretch gently if you need to, and when you're ready... open your eyes.

You are fully grounded and renewed.
Welcome back!
THE MAGIC IS DONE.

Remember you can return to this magical place at any time.

IN A NUTSHELL

Working in harmony with the natural world will help you to balance your energy as you adjust the pace of your life with the cycles and seasons. Listen to your body, rest when you need to, and allow yourself the luxury of longer rest periods in the evenings of the winter months when the days are shorter. The soul still grows in dark and dormant times.

Keep in mind the deep wisdom of the dark. Its riches are priceless. Now let's move on, to fine-tune our connection to the spirit realms and work with the Gods.

12
MAGICAL BONDS

Real intimacy is a sacred experience – John O' Donohue

As we continue our journey, we open ourselves further to the spiritual help available at all times. And like all of the helping spirits, the Gods are a great source of guidance, especially if we treat them as friends. Yes, I said *friends*. Those you can have a laugh and a joke with, who provide a listening ear when you need one. Think about your human friends for a moment. What makes a good friend? Someone you can trust? Someone who accepts you without judgement?

Soul Friends

In the Celtic wisdom tradition, the idea of a soul friend was described by the old Gaelic term, *Anam Ćara*. This was someone who in the early Celtic church would have been a teacher or companion. It was a friendship that transcended all convention, morality and social standing. The Anam Ćara experience is not limited by separation or distance.

It's a meeting of souls where we step into unity with another where there are no barriers. It feeds the ancient yearning our soul has for a sense of belonging. Our magical nature guides us to these soul connections every time.

We all need a soul friend: someone who understands us just as we are. Their love is unconditional, as is our love for them. It is a relationship of reciprocity, harmony and balance between us. When you recognise this in someone, you discover the synchronicities about your lives that deepen your connection.

I have a friend who I met at a spiritual event a few years ago where we had a stall next to each other. I was giving spiritual readings, and my friend was selling her crystal jewellery. We hit it off right from the start and found we had many things in common. And that was just the start. Since that first meeting, we have discovered our lives connect at such deep levels, it's spooky!

We both lost our brothers in tragic circumstances leaving us as the only daughter of our parents. Our brothers' birthdays and death days coincide with our own birthdays in uncanny ways and the synchronicities continue to this day.

I'm sure, like me, you have your own soul friends. The kind of friends you might not see or hear from for ages, and then when you do catch up, it's as if no time has passed at all. You pick up exactly where you left off because the bond is stronger than time and distance. It's unlimited. When we are in the company of kindred spirits, our soul sisters and brothers, we are blessed by the Gods.

Building Relationships

How do we learn to love the Gods in the same way? We treat them with respect for who they are and what they represent. These deities appear in our lives to bring us what we need at the right time. Divine timing is their speciality. They are adepts of the mysteries, standing at every point of the circle of life ready to inspire us with their wisdom.

But the Gods demand something from us in return for their help; it's a two-way relationship. We must be prepared to do something for them.

As personified forms of divine energy, it is natural to want to get up close and personal with a deity. What's the point of keeping someone like the Morrigan at arm's length if we want help with a particular challenge, something which requires courage and discipline?

It's not good enough to only think about a God. If we want to build a relationship with them, we must spend time with them... learning about them, discovering who they are and what they symbolise to us personally. And in return, we offer our thanks, we show our respect. We *honour* them. We take them into our hearts and they show us our own divinity. It's their gift to us.

Sometimes the Gods will show up in your dreams or send you messengers in the form of animals or signs which are sacred to them, e.g. Hekate's keys, Cerridwen's cauldron, the Morrigan's crow or the Dagda's harp. Remember that the language of the Witch is symbolism, and you will open yourself to its magical language in all kinds of synchronistic ways.

Choosing a God or Goddess

How will you serve your chosen deity? I think a good start is to focus on choosing a God or a Goddess who appeals to you, one who resonates... one who feels in harmony with your energy. There are many to choose from, in every spiritual tradition and pantheon you can think of. Keep your heart and mind open to where you feel drawn and whoever calls you.

If we think about it on an energy level, we gravitate towards that which resonates with our vibration. We hit it off with people who are on our wavelength. Why would it be any different with a divine being?

I choose to work with the Morrigan because I feel an affinity with her ways and her traits. I love the fact that she is powerful in all the ways I admire. She is there to help me through the battles of life with her wisdom and tough love. She inspires my creativity with music, and when I connect with her spirit and energy, I find myself in a deeply magical space. It's a place where I experience the spark of fire and fan its flames, where I dance in them with ideas to make them workable and become stories or songs, or a book like this one.

My creativity expresses itself through my connection to this favourite Goddess of mine. She is my muse connecting me to the land, the Otherworld and the magic of my own nature.

A Devotional Practice

Once you have chosen your God or Goddess, it's a good idea to devote some time and space to this divine being who resonates with you. Building an altar will kickstart the process and set the magical wheels in motion for a good relationship between you and your deity.

I have an altar dedicated to the Morrigan, with crow feathers, oracle cards depicting all her animal guises relating to her shapeshifting aspect, a personalised pendant made by a friend, and other meaningful objects. I spend time at my altar, which always begins with lighting a candle and acknowledging the Dark Lady in a prayerful attitude. Just lately, I have been bringing the candle and feather into the office and placing them on my desk before I write. And while my writing is not all about this Goddess, nevertheless making time to be with her sets me up for the work ahead.

Morrigans Prayer

'Morrigans Prayer' is a song I wrote for the Goddess. You can listen to the audio version here: **bit.ly/3JtbTuZ**

Please use it if you choose her as yours.

> *Round the circle three times three*
> *A worthy channel I will be*
> *And all your power into me*
> *Burning bright and flowing free*
> *I roam the battlefields again*
> *Of warrior cries and bleeding men*
> *And on my wings I carry them*
> *The sacred journey home again*
> *I hold you gently to my breast*
> *Peacefully and still you rest*
> *Let no more trials be on your quest*
> *For all you dreams will manifest*
> *Peacefully resting*
> *Morrigans blessing...*

WITCH WAYS
Attunement to Deity

To connect with your chosen God/dess or to *discover who it might be*, here is a practice that will help.

- Make your connection with **solitude, silence** and **stillness.**

- Bring offerings of food and drink appropriate to your chosen deity. If you are not sure who it might be, milk and/or bread will be fine.

- Light a candle and make yourself comfortable.

- Make an offering of a poem, song or a prayer dedicated to your God/dess.

- Focus on your breathing to relax the body.

- When you feel calm and at peace, ask the divine being to step forward and show themselves.

- Ask for a name, a sign, or a symbol.

- Be open and listen. Notice the subtlety of *any* type of communication however it comes through to you.

It's important to bear in mind at this point that the presence of spirit will be different for each one of us. Some people will hear something, perhaps a voice or a sound, music maybe. Others will see a vision or symbols of some kind in the mind. There will be some who feel sensations in their body like a cobweb brushing across their face or a shiver down the spine.

- Observe and stay in the moment. If you don't notice anything, continue to repeat the question and wait patiently.

Remember this is a devotional practice and therefore you will need to devote yourself and your time to the practice of it. If you keep showing up every day, speaking the name of your deity through poem, song or prayer, anything that you offer will have an effect. By the simple act of being present and connecting with a clear intention, the deity will make their presence felt in some way. And if you have to wait, then that also is a test of your devotion. But rest assured they will appear in some way, shape or form.

- How does the presence show up for you?

- Is there a feeling connected with it? Do you feel any particular emotion?

- Does it have a shape, colour or sound? Is there anything specific that defines it?

Record your findings. If you stay with the practice and keep doing the work, you will receive the benefits of it in more ways than you can imagine.

Quite often, I receive ideas spontaneously for a Morrigans Path song, usually while I'm out with my dogs. If I catch the idea quickly enough with a melody or some lyrics, I will record it roughly on my phone and work with it back at home, with a notepad and guitar.

But unless I sit down to work on the idea, it can easily disappear into the ether, and before I know it, I'm absorbed in some household task... one of the joys of working from home. But with some planning, I find that spending a dedicated few hours locked away with an idea, at my Morrigan altar, will reap its rewards, and is how a new song is born. Whatever way you work your magic, a devotional sacred space will add power to your creation or project.

IN A NUTSHELL

Spending time with the Gods will enrich your magical work. You will create a relationship like no other, deepening your connection to the sacred and forging a spiritual bond that strengthens with time.

With a devotional practice to your chosen deity, you can walk between the worlds with confidence and discover the treasures you seek within yourself. They have always been there, but now you know how to find them.

This is how we learn to honour the Gods and find our own divinity.

Do you have your sword and shield at the ready? Now for the magic of the battlefield!

13
WORKING WITH THE WARRIOR

Fear is your teacher, your true adversary, your closest friend – Daniel Allison

We have dreamed about the abundance we seek, climbed the ladder of success in our visions, and ventured into darkness. Now the dim light of the battlefield emerges as conflict arises within us. It's no bad thing. We're growing. Life is an ongoing test of our ability to learn, in whatever way those lessons might present themselves. The magical path is no different, and thankfully, we have the tools of our craft to guide us.

What do we do when challenges arise? Who will help us now?

It's time to do the work of the Warrior. Working with the fiery spirit of Warrior energy prepares us for the inevitable battle that waits around the corner of every bend on the road of *life*. Your work is now Fire orientated, where your enthusiasm and passion for the inner process of transformation comes to the fore. Feel its heat and dance in the flames. It will spur you on to move in the right direction toward those riches you desire.

Passion and Purpose

You may already be armoured with the steely grit of determination, especially if you have dreamed well; your intentions alone will have set the tone of your journey. But now you will have to step boldly out of your comfort zone – the playground of limiting belief – and make your way through the unknown territory of uncertainty. You will know by now that to achieve anything in life, you need to have the will to succeed.

What compels you to do that? What drives you to create?

Whatever your passion is, it will continually push you forwards. It will guide you to improve your output and ability. With dedication and effort, anything can be achieved, but not without a commitment to the work on a consistent basis. Not without *practice*.

Why would it be any different for the Witch or Magician? If you want to work effective magic then you will need to connect with your magical self. The wonderful thing about magic is the support we have from the Otherworld. They're ready and waiting for us to tune in and ask for the help we need. So now we enter the battlefield of the inner planes, and the Warrior leads the way.

Archetypes

The Warrior is an archetypal spirit perfectly aligned with the success and abundance that we seek.

Archetypes are underlying universal patterns based on ancient and primitive energies that over the course of time have become embedded in the human psyche. We all experience these energies on an inner and outer level in our lives, consciously or not. Each stage that we pass through in life can be personified by an archetypal spirit or character, and we find them in myths and legends, films and songs.

Think of a deck of cards. A normal playing deck has four archetypes: king, queen, joker and jack. The tarot has twenty-two archetypes in the form of the major arcana, which are the spiritual blueprint of the Fool and his journey through life.

Life Lessons

Archetypes guide us as we grow. That's their purpose. *The Hero's Journey* was Joseph Campbell's metaphor for the deep, inner journey of transformation; a common template in stories with a hero who goes on an adventure, is victorious in a crisis and returns a changed person.

Birth and death are archetypal patterns that play out in an outward and physical sense and inwardly at a psychic level. We are born and die constantly as we come to the end of different phases of our lives and begin new cycles over and again.

Who Is the Warrior?

The Warrior appears in many stories and fairy tales through the ages, and is one of the primary archetypes. He is virtually identical in every culture. The Warrior transcends gender, as the character traits can be developed in the female as well as the male. Throughout history, it's been portrayed more through the world of men because in general boys and men became warriors and soldiers. But actually, if we think about it, the female warrior has been with us all along too.

At the time of the Celts, feminine figures were deeply associated with their society's preoccupation with war. The warrior culture of the Celts represented the highest caste attainable in their society. It ranked only below the kings, queens and the Druids, who were the judges, teachers and philosophers of the Celtic world.

Warrior Women

Women served as warriors until at least the seventh century. Under old Irish Celtic law, all landowners were required to serve their clans as warriors, and since women had the privilege of owning land, they had an obligation to defend it, which they did. Women were appreciated for their fighting skills and physical prowess as much as for any other attribute they possessed.

Both young women and men aspired to membership in the warrior class, and if they were not born into it through the ownership of land, there was only one other way and that was through fosterage. This was how the young legendary King Arthur, was introduced to his warriorhood status and eventually initiated into his role as king – by the fostering of the mighty Druid Merlin.

Teachers

One of the roles of female warriors was teaching new warriors. It was an old Anglo-Celtic magical belief that teachings flow best from female to male and from male to female. This belief mirrored the Celtic worldview of God and Goddess, male and female, upper world and the Underworld, as two halves of one whole that had to be unified to function properly.

Legends portraying women battle teachers have been preserved in the myths. In Irish mythology, the famous warriors of Ulster known as the Red Branch were taught by the warrior Goddess Scáthach. Her *Isle of Shadow* School of War was located on the Isle of Skye (named after her) in the Hebrides, an island chain off the west coast of mainland Scotland. She was known as a fierce warrior queen, and her alleged leaps and battle yells were said to be a part of her invincible battle teachings reputed to paralyse the enemy with fear.

The Spiritual Warrior

There is no doubt the aspect of Warrior energy will guide us through the physical and active (Earth and Fire) part of life, which is crucial for solving problems and achieving goals. But equally as important, is the emotional and psychological (Water and Air) part of our journey. This is the inner spiritual Warrior, who conquers the greatest enemy of all: the self. The physical Warrior now takes the wisdom they have learned from external battles, to face those internal demons and master themselves.

Self Reliance

All warrior teachings are about self-reliance. The free spirit of the Warrior will push you to step boldly forward on your own and not look back. You must learn to think on your feet and welcome the draw of the challenge ahead. You will need to build strength and courage. You will need to hone the skills of battle.

Are you ready for the challenge? Connecting to your Warrior self will help to face your biggest enemy: fear, to learn its lessons, and transmute it into the higher vibrations of truth and victory, and ultimately love.

To truly love yourself is to know who you really are and honour what you came here to do.

A Magical Guide

This is where your magical guide comes in, to give you the confidence you need to find your true abundance. These are the riches of your magical nature and the true essence of your creative self.

Once you have discovered this, you can integrate the skills of the modern-day Warrior into your everyday life and embrace abundance in all its aspects. You will learn the art of swordcraft to cut away all negative energy so that you can honour your true self. You will also learn the art of shield craft to neutralise any harmful energies: your psychic protection.

As a result of working with the Warrior, you will eventually discover the peaceful Warrior within and know how to stand in the power of that energy. For only when you have made peace with the conflict that rages through your mind and body will you find the riches of your soul.

The Morrigan

Now is the time to work with the warrior spirit, to embrace the energy and become it. We're going to continue to work with the Morrigan, a true warrior goddess. Invoke her spirit and you will be transformed by the fierce and magnificent energy of a Goddess who takes no prisoners.

In the most challenging of times, the Dark Lady has been by my side, prompting and guiding, and providing an inner strength I didn't know I had. She is the Celtic embodiment of victory, and of the strength and power of the divine feminine.

It was common for a Goddess in Celtic stories to be expressed in different guises. It was a way of demonstrating more of her qualities. Here are some of the Morrigan's many different guises:

- Shape-Shifter
- Faery Queen
- Goddess of Sovereignty
- Seeress
- Sorceress

- Phantom Queen
- Lover
- Earth Mother
- Liminal Goddess
- Prophetess

The Morrigan is predominately known as queen of battle and death, and one of the most powerful Celtic deities. Wherever there is battle and strife in Celtic mythology, you will find the Morrigan. As a Goddess of war, she was called upon by the Celts to bring them victory on the battlefield. She evolved from a cultural need to protect the land and all that is held dear, out of the need for justice and to bring balance. Therefore, as a Sovereign deity and protector of the land (she is the land itself!), she asks us what in life is worth fighting for.

Take a moment to contemplate what that means in your own life. What do you care enough to fight for?

Write it down and let the words flow. You might surprise yourself.

Victory

Celtic war deities reflected the type of warfare of their culture and much of Irish warfare revolved around cattle raids. Cattle were perceived as a great source of wealth and were used as currency to pay debts and bride prices. This is why the Morrigan is often linked to cattle raids in the old stories, as a Goddess of Sovereignty and the land and its wealth. She is either stealing cattle, herding them or making it difficult for others to obtain them; all functions reflecting the cosmology of Celtic warfare!

The Morrigan is the spirit of revolution and the overthrowing of the old order to embrace a brighter future. She is the symbol of directed aggression and the power to score victory at any cost. You may not be in the military where you find yourself serving on the actual physical battlefield, but that doesn't mean you won't need a fierce and mighty battle queen to help you fight your battles. The Morrigan will help to build your inner strength, conquer your demons and inspire you in your darkest moments.

WITCH WAYS
A Dedicated Altar

Make an altar to honour the Morrigan by placing symbolic objects representing all the traits and characteristics of the warrior. Think strength, courage, confidence… You may have a picture or a statue of the Goddess. I have a pendant that an artist friend of mine created with a picture painted of the Dark Lady on it. She made it for me especially, and I wear it whenever I'm singing with Morrigans Path as my own way of honouring the Goddess. As an example, I have used that on a dedicated altar to the Morrigan, with crow feathers and a piece of beautiful slate I brought back from a Morrigan sacred tattoo retreat in Wales a few years ago.

Ian and I were invited to the retreat to play our music, and I ran a Warrior Woman workshop which was great fun. They had a tattoo artist and priestess of the Morrigan over from America with the longest, brightest red hair who performed an embodiment of the Goddess. It was an interesting, theatrical performance. The rest of the time, the flame-haired priestess held sacred tattoo rituals in a hall on the site.

I remember walking past the hall one day to the sound of thunderous drumming which continued for hours through each ritual from beginning to end. That's the closest I've ever come to having a tattoo myself, but it seemed a mighty long time to be sitting and having your ears blasted, so I never did venture in.

Honouring The Morrigan

Animals associated with the Morrigan include the raven and the crow, the wolf, the eel, the cow and the horse. These are the forms she takes in the Irish myths and can be seen in her shapeshifting guises. Collect any symbols that you associate with these animals and add them to your altar. Where I live, there is a huge crow population, and consequently, crow feathers have a habit of coming home from my walks, to be hung in the Treehouse or placed on the altars in our house indoors.

Gather what you can to represent and honour this wild and dark Goddess. Anything that reminds you of the Morrigan will have value and serve as a link to her energy and spirit. Make your offerings with food and drink if you wish. I prefer to sing and send out prayers. But if you have none of these things to hand when your need is great, the *greatest* offering will be your loyal presence.

Now let's meet Her!

A Journey to the Battlefield

Listen to the audio version here: **bit.ly/3NqIVwN**

Make your connection to your magical self and the Otherworld with **solitude** and **stillness**.

- Use deep, slow breathing to relax... releasing all the tension in your body and calming your mind.
- Imagine putting down roots of golden light into the earth, travelling deeper into the ground with every breath. Take in the earth's energy, feel it glowing and flowing around your body, its golden light warming and filling every cell... and let it flow out through the

soles of your feet like roots spreading back into the earth.

- Give no attention to your thoughts; let them come and go like passing traffic.

- Engage all your senses, and remember that what you see and hear and what you smell and feel will add power to your experience… building the images around you as you go.

- Feel the energy flow increasing as you open your mind and shift your focus from the outside world to the inner planes and your third eye centre.

Visualise a doorway leading out of the room… open it and walk through it, closing it behind you. You are surrounded by a heavy mist, and walking slowly through it, you smell the dampness of the earth, and hear the shrieking of crows.

The mist gradually begins to clear, revealing a vast and open plain, with a great expanse of pale blue sky all around you. Your stomach churns from an overpowering stench, and you stare in horror at the crows feasting on the bloodied corpses of men and women, swords and shields scattered around them.

Among the mounds of bodies lying across the land, you can see a figure walking towards you: a tall woman dressed in black leather, her exposed skin covered in the bright tattoos of war. Her face is smeared with black and red markings, and she is looking straight at you as she removes a leather headdress and lays it down among the warriors.

Her long black hair is plaited tightly around her head, and dark red streaks of blood splatter her cheeks and throat. She is carrying a short double-edged sword in one hand, and as she draws closer, her dark eyes flash at you.

Your heart is pounding and you're unable to move or speak. Who is she?

'I am the dark maiden of the night, the mother of war, here to take the souls of these warriors home. You will know me as many things, and that's because I am all of them.'

She points to the dead with her sword. 'These are my children, who answered the call... and with courage and strength fought with every breath. Fearless until the last. And now... for the final journey, I carry them home.

Are you ready to take to the battlefield, Magical One? Are you willing to give your life for the riches you seek? Will you raise your sword to cut down whatever stands in the way, will you carry your shield close to your heart, guarding its treasure? When you can do this, when you are ready and willing... when you are primed for conflict and will take up your arms, I will be there beside you.'

You look at this formidable woman and ask, 'Who are you, really?'

She lays her sword down and looks up at the crows circling overhead, and you follow her gaze. You look back to find the woman is no longer there... there's no sign of her. But a large raven, perched on the handle of her sword, is there instead, in her place. It flaps its wings and shrieks loudly, staring at you, sending a cold shiver up your spine.

You cannot take your eyes off the blue sheen of its feathers... you *feel* its knowing presence. And as you continue to watch it, it grows bigger right in front of you. Stepping back, you make room for the raven, and the bird continues to call out as it becomes as large as the battlefield itself.

You watch the other giant crows as they swoop down upon the bodies of the slain, lifting them in their beaks and placing them gently upon the wings of the great bird. As the crows place the dead warriors on the raven's back, a rainbow light emerges around each one as their physical body fades... while the raven glows with every colour of the rainbow. You have never seen such a vision before, and gasp as the bird pulsing with light, takes off from the battlefield and soars into the vast

expanse of sky above you. Your legs give way as you fall to the ground, and everything goes dark...
    Morrigans Prayer ~ Morrigans Path

Pause for a few minutes

Gradually the light comes back... and you are watching the great raven grow smaller as it flies through the clouds above and disappears. You realise you're standing now, and look down at your feet to see they are clad in soft black leather. The same black leather covers your body, and your bare arms and hands are covered in bluey-black raven tattoos. You raise a hand to touch a thick braid of your hair, and notice your other hand carries a shield covering your heart. On the ground at your feet lies a sword, and you pick it up, feeling the weight of it. You can hold it easily.

Holding the shield close to your chest, you lift the sword to the sky... feeling a shock of energy coursing through your body... and you cry out to the wind as it blows around you. You are held steady by a power you have never known until now. You are strong and determined; you are ready and willing to do whatever you need to do. You will honour yourself, fight for freedom and stand for justice in all things. You will find the peace inside you and be guided by it... back home, again and again, returning to the arms of the one who holds you.

'I am the dark maiden of the night, the mother of war...the crone of death and rebirth... I walk beside you, always. You are my child of battle, the one who falls and rises again and again. You are the Warrior.'

The mist surrounds you once more and clings to your skin. The dampness of the earth rises up and the shrieking of crows fills the air. Walking with great purpose through the mist, you enter the door and find yourself back in the room.

- Follow your breath as you draw up the earth's energy with each inhalation and exhale the memory of your experience.

- Refreshed and fully awake, you are becoming aware of your physical body. Refreshed and fully awake now... you are becoming aware of your physical body.

- Wriggling your fingers and toes, stretch gently if you need to, and when you're ready... open your eyes.

You are fully grounded in the energy of the Warrior. Welcome back.
THE MAGIC IS DONE.

IN A NUTSHELL

Tuning into your Warrior nature prepares you for success, whatever your idea of that may be. The Morrigan will guide you through the battlefield of life to victory and the ultimate goal of peace within yourself. She is an incredibly magical deity to experience and learn from. But there are others from history and mythic tales that you can also work with: Boudicca – the historical queen of the Iceni, Cúchulain – the legendary Irish Celtic Warrior, Arthur Pendragon, Warrior King of the Britons, to name but a few.

Work with your guide and you will never feel alone on the battlefield again. Remember, the fear of becoming who you really are is the cause of any resistance and separation from your power in the first place. Strike it out. Claim your sovereignty.

The Warrior lives in you.

14
PROSPER WITH THE SUN

Ô sunlight! The most precious gold to be found on earth – Roman Paye

It's time to let the sunshine in. Working with the cycles of the sun helps to guide us as we dive deep and tap into our manifesting powers. Here's the gold you've been looking for.

Whereas the moon is about illusion, mystery, and illumination, the sun is about radiance, clarity, and optimism, directing our energy outwards and working magic through our actions and deeds.

Who Is the Sun?

Let's look at the magical aspects of the sun. It's a good way to get a feel for the spirit and energy of this amazing ball of fire in our skies!

The sun is Lord of the Day, radiating outwards and dispelling the darkness with the bright light of optimism, bringing clarity and a zest for life. His healing rays warm the dampest of spirits with life-giving energy. He represents the masculine principle (yang) of communication and positive action and is the bearer of good news and accomplishment.

His appearance heralds a time of increase and moving ahead with plans to bring success in all personal achievements in the spirit of fun and excitement. The teachings of the sun are many, but in general, they bring a sunny outlook and a warm heart for your journey.

Think about it. The vitality and feel-good factor of the sun lights up your pathway. The benefits of working with solar energy will bring the power of increase into your life on every level. This spiritual aspect of tuning into the sun's energy helps the soul to blossom, just as it acts upon the earth in nature. It radiates from within and connects you to an abundant source of positive and vibrant energy, enriching your life and enabling you to embrace every opportunity as it shows up.

Sun Cycles

The daily cycle of the sun rising in the east each day and setting in the west is closely related to the seasonal cycle of crops planted in the Spring and harvested in the Autumn. The agricultural cycle is entirely dependent on the annual cycle, as the crops grow with the waxing power of the sun from Spring to Summer, and after harvesting their yield will die back in the Autumn with the waning power of the sun.

The great thing about working magic with the sun is that, unlike the moon, we don't have to wait a whole month before the particular phase that we need comes around. The sun's daily cycle is much more convenient if you have less time, and need to get cracking with your spellwork. Bearing in mind the sun's annual cycle, you can align with the lighter and darker times of the year for increasing and decreasing power in your witchery.

Daily Phases

- Sunrise
- Early morning: 8 am until noon

- Noon
- Early afternoon: 1- 3 pm
- Late afternoon: 3 - sunset
- Sunset

WITCH WAYS
Good Morning!

Waking up and rising to the idea of success and prosperity in your life is greatly supported by the sunrise on a daily basis. Every day when you wake up, just being grateful for that, will influence your energy and set in motion the changes needed to bring about the riches you seek. It sounds too simple to be a practice but do *not* underestimate the power of gratitude. This is something you will find expanding and growing within these pages, and that is because at the heart of your spiritual power is gratitude for all your abundance.

Beginning your day in gratitude is working magic on yourself. It's a transformative act and will change your life. Believe that, and you will see evidence of it cropping up in all aspects of your life: your relationships, your health, your creativity and your finances.

From now on, the moment you wake up in the morning, be glad you have. There are many who don't. How fortunate are you to be here to live another day?

Rise Up to Riches

At sunrise, go outside into nature (a garden or a park), somewhere you can see the horizon clearly, facing the east, and watch that magnificent ball of fire ascending in the sky. Feast your eyes on the colours as they spread over the horizon and watch the magic of nature in action. It's a truly amazing phenomenon don't you think? And it happens *every single day*.

Imagine you are seeing through the eyes of one who is witnessing it for the first time. Now is the time to connect with your inner child. Think of all the things you have to be glad about. As you ponder on these thoughts and feel them in your heart, sense a smile spreading from the heart and around the rest of your body. As the sun rises, raise both arms, feeling your smile creep across your face. How good does that feel? This solar power brings you life; it brings you the spark of creation and feeds your soul with its life-giving energy.

Take that power into your body and absorb it through every cell. Feel its radiance within. Acknowledge it as the source of all life, and see its rays illuminating the whole planet. Allow its spirit to fill you with energy and a fresh perspective.

Say or sing this chant:

> *Star of fire, rays of light*
> *Keeper of all power bright*
> *Spark of life and sacred flame*
> *Shine in me and out again*

Thank the sun for its wisdom and go about your day.

Morning Sun

Now we are continuing in the flow of energy at sunrise. The morning is a good time to reset your magical work for the increase of energy wherever it's needed. However the weather is playing out and even if you cannot see the sun, you know that it's still there, behind those clouds. Name your desire and set your intention.

A Wealthy Witch Walk

Take a Witch Walk and dedicate your exercise to the sun and its power in your pocket, the realm of your finances. Focus on that thought, and walk. Concentrate on every step you take and see it as increasing the money in your life and bringing you financial freedom. This is not a time for judgment or negativity. You must override any feelings of lack, and work with a willingness to improve this area of your life. No matter how much or little is in your bank account, the key factor is your attitude toward it.

The Magician works with their will (desires) to direct their energy (thoughts) out into the world. This is the underlying principle, the rock-solid foundation of your own witchery at work. This is what you are building on all the time. Your *willingness* to become a more abundant, wealthy, and prosperous Witch in every way is the first step on your road to riches. Make every one of those steps count. Do the work of one who knows their own mind, keeps it open to each opportunity as it arises and devotes the time every single day to the power of focused intention.

Magic is not something you only do at weekends or when you (think you) have the time. It's a practice and a lifestyle. A way of *being*. Do you want to bring riches into your life? Roll your sleeves up, brush the cobwebs out of your mind, and get to work on yourself.

Work with this chant while you walk:

The more I learn, the way is clearer
The more I earn is getting nearer
The more I learn, the more I earn!

You can really get into a good rhythm with those words, build it into a brisk pace, and even fit in a few dance steps. And yes, if you want to know, I do that myself when I'm out on the sea wall. The important thing is that you enjoy your chanting and develop a feel for what you're singing about.

When you combine the voice, with walking or dancing and a focused magical intention, you are creating magic at the atomic level. Every cell of your body is alive with the idea, and as you bring it into form through your actions, you make the invisible a visible thing.

The power of your Witch Walk is in your focus and repetition of the mantra while walking. It will kickstart your day for prospering on every level. Observe how many blades of grass you can see around you as you walk, and how much soil is beneath your feet. That's natural abundance. Mother Nature is teeming with life-giving offerings, and if we take the time to notice her gifts, she works her magic on us, through us, and out into the world.

Midday Magic

When the sun is at its highest peak in the sky is a great time to turbo-charge your magic. You can tap into this power to charge up your tools and yourself with the high energy of noon.

Gather your divination tools: any stones, cards, runes, or pendulums that you use, and place them outside under the midday sun. Leave them out for a good couple of hours to charge up, a bit like plugging a digital device into a wall socket. Except this is your solar socket!

Depending on what time of year it is and where you are in the world, it can be a good time to sunbathe. But remember that over-exposure to the sun's rays when it's at its strongest is not a good thing. Being sensible and using your common sense goes without saying... beware of frying yourself at noon and take all the precautions you need to protect yourself.

On an inner level, burnout from too much sun energy can literally send you into meltdown. Its causes are unrealistic expectations, and the symptoms are being over-ambitious, volatile, and overwhelming others *and* yourself, into the bargain.

By the same token, you can benefit from some winter midday sunshine and recharge your energy just as well. The temperature is irrelevant; it's the position and phase of the sun that matters.

The Flame of Inspiration

Inspiration is a feeling that injects us with the urge and the ability to do something creative. To help boost your manifesting power with the midday sun, spend some time in focused contemplation about your creativity. For example, I need the power of inspiration to continue to write this book. When I am inspired, it motivates me to get on with the job and finish it. I find the stamina I need to endure the long hours of writing when I am motivated by the power of inspiration.

If you focus on your creativity and are open to receiving every way that inspiration can reach you, it will appear through all kinds of opportunities. The fire in our heads, the spark of inspiration, lights up the way for us to create whatever we want, and the spirit of the sun is a perfect ally and guide for encouraging the muse to show up.

In this case, the muse *is* the sun.

Meeting the Muse

Listen to the audio version here: **bit.ly/3plykLK**

Begin your connection to your magical self with **solitude** and **stillness.**

- Make yourself comfortable outside in the sunshine or

somewhere indoors where you can feel the sun on your face.

- Ponder on the idea of financial freedom; the thought of not having to rely on anyone or anything else to provide you with the means to live the life you really want to live. Know that it's *absolutely possible* that you can have this freedom of choice when you accept it as a truth in your mind and heart.

- Feel the sunshine on your face and the spark of a small flame inside of you. This is the rekindling of something that has always been with you before you came into the world and will remain with you when you leave. This is the source of your own spiritual power brought to you by the rays of the sun.

- Open up to the rays as they pass through every thread of thought, filling your head with light. This is the light that shines on your dream, a vision so strong that it's completely visible in your waking moments. Right now, it's revealed to you as you are led across the threshold from the visible realms to the world of the invisible.

- Allow the sun to show the way, to shine its light on your path and take you where you need to go...

Your journey takes you along a path through the countryside and into a field of sunflowers blazing in golden hues of light. You narrow your eyes against the bright glare as a radiant figure takes form in front of you and begins to speak:

'Shield yourself if you must, Magical One, my energy is strong and vibrant. But it will give you great clarity if you can learn to use it to your advantage. I shine to let you know that all is possible and there is nothing that cannot manifest if you believe it to be so... if you can accept that it's yours before it takes form.

Your journey is clear now, and it progresses because *you* have progressed. You have learned to connect with the light within, and so it radiates out and leads you onwards. This light of your inner sacred flame is your desire to create, succeed, and grow in all aspects of yourself and your life.

Bathe in it, take it and act upon it. Rejoice in your new-found freedom and rich bounty; it's all there. Revel in me and delight in the warmth of every opportunity, for each one is golden. However, beware the scorch of my dazzling rays, for too much of a good thing cancels itself out.

Night follows day, yin and yang, the Lord and Lady... balance in all things.'

You are filled with a glow that spreads warmly around your body, and your mind expands outwards. An idea begins to take form in your mind... a quickening. You know what you need to do and feel compelled to move on it, to take action. You have abilities and skills. Why wouldn't you want to share your gifts?

Turning this over in your mind, you feel enthusiasm growing inside you and an urge to share your idea with others.

Meanwhile, the radiant being speaks once more.

'Now is the time to embrace the light of inspiration, to ask what it will create, what it will do for you and for others. How will you prosper from its expansion in your life? Breathe it in, Magical One, and feel it charging every cell in your body. Feel into my energy and ask what it will do for you. I am listening...'

PAUSE FOR A FEW MINUTES

'The light becomes you, and you become the light. This is your success – discovering the treasure inside you – a golden opportunity that cannot help but reach out beyond itself and enrich all those it touches. Enjoy and prosper from your discoveries!'

The radiant being moves out of focus and fades into the distance, but you feel its bright and warming presence staying with you. Nurture these feelings and notice how they grow and radiate outwards. Watch them shining out into the world.

Feel the rays as they pass through every thread of thought, filling your head with light. This is the light that shines on your dream, a vision so strong that it's completely visible, in your waking moments.

Right now, it remains with you as you journey back out of the sunflower field and onto the path through the countryside. And finally, you cross the threshold from the invisible realms to the world of the visible once again.

You are back in the room.

- Breathe in deeply and draw up the earth's energy, and breathe out the memory of your experience.

- Refreshed and fully awake, you are becoming aware of your physical body. Refreshed and fully awake now...you are becoming aware of your physical body.

- Wriggling your fingers and toes, stretch gently if you need to, and when you're ready... open your eyes.

You are fully grounded in the energy of prosperity.
Welcome back.
THE MAGIC IS DONE.

On this journey of abundance, you know that enthusiasm and joy will put fuel in your tank. How good does it feel? How inspired are you now?

Write down your answers. What have you resolved to do and be? What do you believe you can have in your life?

This is your own creative process in action.... manifesting through the power of your words and grounding your ideas into form.

Good Afternoon!

As you harness, shape and direct the energy for magic, attuning to solar power in the afternoon will focus your efforts on anything that requires clarity and resolution. That makes it a good time for communication, professional matters, and balancing the bank account.

Although the sun's power is waning at this stage, the fact that the energy is still strong and warm makes it more versatile than the waning lunar energies. As well as the more direct midday solar energy we have used for inspiration and magnification, we can still boost our magical efforts but with a focus on strategy and exploration.

If you want to work magic for travel and adventure, get out in the afternoon and cast a sun spell. It's time to put those plans into action.

Spell for Empowerment in Your Career

Isn't it interesting that the solar plexus chakra point is depicted as yellow? This is the place of our personal power and houses the inner sun that we can connect to at any time. Personal power is an energy we nurture with healthy self-esteem and belief and faith in the self. It grows as we learn to honour who we are.

Working with a sun deity with the intention of strengthening your personal power is a useful daily practice you can include in your witchery. When you have the inner strength that comes from honouring yourself, your Witch work will benefit, and your magic will be more effective because your belief is the underlying principle that gives it credence.

We're going to work with Apollo, the Greek sun God, and bay leaves. Our purpose here is to encounter the masculine principle, which works through both men and women to move us toward a goal. With the power of the afternoon sun and the magic of Apollo, we will experience clarity, optimism and renewed trust in any project we are working on.

TRY THIS:

Think about the idea of professionalism in your area of magical and creative expertise. You may be an artist, a writer, an artisan or a craftsperson. You may be a holistic therapist, an herbalist, a teacher or a spiritual reader. You may already have your own business or you might have a vision of wanting to turn your passion into a vocation.

YOU WILL NEED:

- The Sun tarot card
- A sunstone crystal
- A few bay leaves and a pen
- A tea light

WHAT TO DO:

- Prop up your Sun card and place your sunstone on your altar.
- Write on a separate bay leaf each of these words: **foresight, faith** and **purpose**.
- Place the bay leaves and sunstone around the Sun card.
- Light the candle.
- Visualise your intention to become stronger and see

yourself empowered in your chosen field.

- Spend some time looking at the picture in front of you with soft focus vision, using the power of your breath to relax and become passive.

- When your eyes begin to feel tired – close them.

- Ask the spirit of Apollo to impress upon you all you need to know.

- Visualise the sun god coming to life in your imagination. Do not underestimate the invisible power of the imagination, it is the doorway to the inner planes.

- Trust in the process.

- Now mentally step into the picture and see yourself in it. Give yourself a wave! Now actually *feel* yourself in the picture and take a good look around you. What do you see? Hear? Smell? Touch something in your surroundings... how does it feel?

- As your experience becomes more lucid, the sun God will begin to communicate with you. Be open to any impressions you receive through your psychic senses. They may appear loud and clear to your physical senses, or you may be aware on a far more subtle level.

- You may be given or shown something symbolic and relevant. If you're unsure of its meaning, ask for more information.

- Be passive and receptive. This opens you up as a channel to communicate with Apollo... and don't be surprised when he talks back!

- Acknowledge his presence and listen.

- Remember all that you can and bring the knowledge back with you. Did he expand on the words you wrote on the leaves? Were there any more words that he gave you?

- When you have received your answers, thank the sun God and gradually withdraw from your surroundings in the card and become aware of your body and breath.

- When you are grounded back fully into physical awareness, open your eyes and write down your experience.

- Burn the bay leaves and bury the ash in the ground.

THE MAGIC IS DONE.

Now contemplate those three words: foresight, faith and purpose. How do they relate to your work? Do you feel any different about your line of business after your chat with Apollo? Has it inspired you to take action in any way?

I work a lot with his energy to empower my creative ability with music, writing and the healing aspects of my work.

Aligning your intentions with the afternoon sun will strengthen your connection to the Gods and your inner sun.

Sunset

Much like the waning moon phase, as the sun goes down, it's a good time to put your magical efforts into anything that you want to decrease in your life. Reducing or removing completely that which does not serve you anymore is an energetic clearance you can do on a daily basis. A bad habit that you want to break, the weight you want to lose, an addiction, anything, in fact, that you want to release and let go of will all benefit from a bit of sunset magic.

Here are some useful sunset practices to do:

THE VISUAL

Face west and watch the changing colour of that ball of fire as it descends on the horizon. As the sun goes down, see and feel the energy of your habit or addiction draining into the earth.

THE PHYSICAL

This is a great time for grounding, so if you do yoga, get on your mat and do some gentle stretches and pranayama (breathwork) to ground the energy of your day back into the earth.

When you're feeling wired and burned out, take a Witch Walk, fill your steps with the energy of release and cast your specific intention to the setting sun. A good night's sleep does wonders too!

THE VOCAL

Light a candle, and hold a piece of smoky quartz. Say or sing this chant:

> *Setting sun as you go down*
> *Take my fears away*
> *Bury them into the ground*
> *At the break of day*

Repeat this mantra and feel your energy clearing. Write down all those fears that you want to release... burn them, and either bury the ash, cast it out into the wind or a natural body of water.

IN A NUTSHELL

Work your prosperity magic from sunrise to midday for expanding and growing, and from the afternoon onwards to sunset for decreasing and releasing all that stands in your way of being prosperous. With these practices, you will see how the sun and the seed of life as illustrated in the daily and yearly solar cycles are so closely related, and how in past times the Gods of the sun and the crops were seen as one.

Honouring the sun connects us to our ancestors as we celebrate the greatest mystery of life... birth and death. The idea that we are born and pass on to another life where we reincarnate again into the physical, is a theme that unites many religions and spiritual traditions.

Contemplate this great mystery while tuning into the daily solar cycle to increase every golden opportunity for success and prosperity.

FINDING GOLD

15
MONEY CONSCIOUSNESS

Prosperity results when we balance the outflow with the inflow – Diana Cooper

Your money mindset is the root of all your financial good. The relationship you have with money determines how it plays out in your life. Are you willing to accept that you can have the financial freedom you want before it manifests for you?

Whatever that relationship has been like up until now, if you want to, you can change it. It doesn't matter what it was like when you were growing up, what your parents thought about money or how they handled it. Yes, there are factors that have contributed to your current identity and attitude toward money, and they will have an influence on the way in which you perceive it and handle it. But none of that controls you or has the final say in your financial success, now, or in the future. What you create from here is up to you.

Taking Responsibility

You get to decide how your relationship with money will be. What does that look like for you? Think about what your desires and values are around finances. Get really clear about what you want *specifically*. Having enough to live on and having more than enough to live on are two different things. Both will depend on *how* you want to live and what your needs and desires are.

Remember, we're talking about abundance here.

The key is to develop a healthy mindset around money and master the art of managing it. We must also learn to use it wisely, and learn how to create it so that we can benefit from its gifts. The freedom it gives you when it flows abundantly *is* a gift because you can do so much more when you have choices. Money determines your options.

However, your financial health is an inside job, and that's where you must focus if you want to create good relations with money. Become its friend, treat it with respect and it will pay off. Literally. Developing a positive self-image is fundamental. And as the way you think, talk and behave toward yourself improves, so will your finances.

Try this writing practice:

- How much more positive can you be about the way you think, feel and talk about money?

- What do you need and want to spend your money on?

- Are you (feeling) worthy of what you want?

Explore these questions, contemplate their meanings, and ponder your answers. Write it all down. The more specific you can be, the more precise will be the response from your own natural wisdom. As you become clearer about the part money plays in your life, the stronger your sense of responsibility toward it becomes.

The Law of Flow

To get to grips with the money in our life, we must look at it from an energy perspective to understand the law of flow. Our money is like the air and blood supply within our bodies. It has to keep moving and flowing. Healthy circulation is crucial. If it gets stuck in one place, the energy will stagnate. And like a pond with no outflow, the water becomes murky and stinks. What does your cash flow look like? Are your incomings in balance with your outgoings?

If you struggle with keeping your bank balance the right way around, start making changes toward financial health with a few minor adjustments:

- Keep a simple records book and make sure you are living within your means and not spending more than you are earning.

- Be vigilant about your money self-talk.

- Take a money management class or seek financial advice from a professional or wise friend.

Look after your money and it will look after you. Money self-care creates a healthy flow of energy in your life and leads the way to success.

Becoming Professional

When you take the time to nourish your passions first, you will find you have more than enough to help nourish others.

When our boys were very young, I can remember toys all over the floor, a toddler wobbling around in a walker and another baby rolling around on the floor, while I played my guitar and wrote songs in between nappy changes and feed times. And no, it didn't happen *all* the time! I snatched those magical moments among the mundane trials of messy feeds and bodily functions. It all went into the cauldron.

When the boys went to school, I studied and learned everything I could about spirituality and Witchcraft, and gradually I developed the skills I needed to earn from what I loved to do. Transferring the skills of a teacher of horse and rider, to becoming a professional tarot reader and a healer have all grown from the persistence to keep doing what I love doing. And that is my biggest message to you, dear Magical One.

You too can turn your passions into a profession, and if you are already doing that, I salute you.

Ask yourself the question: Am I doing as much as I can for myself in order to serve my customers, readers, clients, and/or students? In other words, are you continuing to improve yourself as a professional? Are you investing in expanding and improving *your* knowledge and experience so that you are better equipped to help others?

With the amount of free content available nowadays, information and knowledge are affordable for *everyone*. The currency is time and commitment. I have learned from teachers and books and by practising my craft by myself and with others. I have read cards for friends for free, played gigs for charity, and written for free, and it has all been *worth it*. We have to earn the right to charge for what we do, and we do it through training and serving as an apprentice in our chosen field.

I have worked my way up from taking courses and coaching from others to doing the same *for others*, but it has taken time… many years, in fact. And only in recent years have I been able to pay for any of that.

But I can tell you the time and effort are paying off. *I am enriching my life.*

You can do that too.

You don't need a lot of money to start with. You just need to believe in yourself and work and live with the idea of being, doing and having *whatever* you desire. I have lived with the idea of prosperity, success and abundance for a long time; but it's been a slow burn. It takes time to make your dreams a reality.

WITCH WAYS
A Money Letter

Here is a spell to raise your money vibration and kickstart the process of claiming it as yours.

It's time to get pen and paper out and write a letter of thanks to the universe.

TRY THIS TEMPLATE OR CREATE YOUR OWN:

> *Dear Abundant Universe,*
> *Thank you so much for the cash refund, I really appreciate it!*
> *I've helped others in my life and have done so with love and kindness, but have never before thought of it in terms of money. As money is energy, I am asking for a refund of all the energy I have given over the years and am grateful for the opportunity to do so.*
> *I love and believe in myself, and I love and believe in others.*
> *I know the world is abundant and that I am worthy and entitled to a cash refund.*
> *Thank you so much for the £/$/€ ....*
> *With love and gratitude, [Yourself]*

- If you have a dedicated room for magical work, place the letter in the southwest corner along with a tea light and any other sacred or power objects you have.

- If you don't have a room especially, place it in the southwest corner of your home.

- Visit your sacred space daily, light the candle, and re-read your letter to the universe while pondering the imminent arrival of your refund.

- Expect a nice surprise, know that it's on its way, and see it as already in your hands.

THE MAGIC IS DONE.

Remember energy-wise, what you put out comes back to you. You are absolutely worthy of this refund.

Meeting Your Rich & Future Self

Imagine it's five years from now. See yourself having received all the things you desire at this present moment in your life. Know that you have achieved what you are setting out to do now.

- Close your eyes and breathe in deeply… exhaling slowly until you begin to feel calm and peaceful.

- Focus on a bright light pulsing at your third eye centre. Breathe in the light and breathe out into it… see it expanding and becoming brighter.

- As you look into the light, you see a silhouetted figure walking towards you… getting bigger.

- As the figure draws closer, you recognise yourself. You are smiling and happy.

- Ask this future you a question: *What is my priority right now, regarding money?*

- Take your time... and believe in what you are hearing as your future self gives you an answer.

- Then ask:

How can I fully follow my heart?
How can I hold the vision of what I want and take one step at a time toward the future of my own riches?

- Spend as much time as you need, listening to and absorbing the wisdom of your future self.

- Give thanks and bid yourself goodbye... watching the figure becoming smaller as it walks away into the light.

- Breathe deeply and slowly to ground yourself back into the physical body.

- When you are fully back in the room, write down the answers you were given and anything else about your experience.

This is a powerful and useful practice that you can return to again and again. Connecting to your soul's wisdom and learning to trust in its guidance will strengthen your faith and belief in the power of who you came here to be, available to you across space and time.

IN A NUTSHELL

You have to accept that you can have the things you desire *before* they can manifest in your life. This applies to your pocket as well as anything else. Financial health requires the same TLC that your physical, mental and emotional health does. Give it the attention it deserves, make your intention to improve what you can and that old friend *transformation* will show up in droves.

The magic of money is all about harmonious change. On a vibrational level, remember that you attract what you are and not what you want. You may want to be wealthy, but if you're not thinking and acting in harmony with the energetic frequency of wealth… it ain't happening!

Move into alignment with your desires, act accordingly and you will *begin* to manifest them as your reality.

16
THE LESSONS OF MONEY

Transforming our relationship to money is possible and it is necessary – Jessie Susannah Karnatz, 'The Money Witch'

Money teaches us many things. For centuries it has been used as a symbol of power and it's not hard to see how that has come about and how our sense of personal value has been tied to money. And that is my point. There is an attachment to the stuff and it's undeniable: money can, if we let it, rule our lives.

How we earn money and make it is very much determined by our attitude towards it, even though we might not even be conscious of that most of the time. What would happen if we did have that awareness? When my parents told me all those years ago, that I couldn't have a pony because there wasn't enough money, what did that teach me? That money was limited... and there wasn't *enough*.

How we receive money into our lives is determined by and relative to how we perceive it. How does money come to you? Think about it. Are you happy with the situation? And does it provide you with enough money to live on?

That in itself is a tricky question. What is enough? What one person perceives as enough may not be another's way of seeing it. Without going into a minefield of analytics here, it's fair to say that if we want to change our minds around money, we must look at both the inner work and the outer work to be done. The inner work involves our thoughts, feelings, beliefs and attitudes about ourselves and money, while the outer work is more about how we manage it in our lives and how we market ourselves and promote our message.

There is no getting away from the fact that despite how much or little money we have, until we address whatever internal blocks we have on the matter, we will continue to self-sabotage our success in this area of our life. And now you see how we are constantly returning to how we feel about ourselves and the value we place upon who we are and where we've come from. That old boomerang of self-worth.

The Witch Wound

The Witch Wound is a soul wound embedded deep inside the human psyche. If you have any fears around empowerment and money, you are not alone. It could be that you made a vow of poverty or something similar in a past life, or that ancestral trauma has been passed down in your bloodlines. These things influence us on a deeply subconscious level and reflect in our outer world and current incarnation.

What Is It?

The Witch Wound is a term coined by writer, Kimberley Jones, over twenty years ago. However, it's been around for centuries. It's a personal and collective scar originating from the Burning Times, a 300-year period of persecution and execution of predominantly women (some men and children) wrongly accused of witchcraft. The wound is ancestral or past-life trauma, a deep cellular memory carried down through the generations and perpetuated by a patriarchal society.

For centuries the Witches and Wise Ones have healed with plants, midwifed the living and the dying, counselled lost souls, read messages in the stars, channelled spirits, and honoured the cycles of nature. We have *cared* for the earth and each other. And yet for hundreds of years, many were singled out and suffered intolerance and persecution. They were hunted, tortured, hung, burned and drowned on account of their gender, religion, ethnicity, or social standing.

Any kind of oppression and discrimination is unacceptable. But to be persecuted for *sharing* these magical gifts with our fellow humans is a crime against humanity (thank the Gods for the ferocious divine feminine).

How Does It Manifest?

The Witch Wound manifests as a form of disempowerment that prevents us from allowing our gifts to shine and speak our truth. It can show up as insecurity, lack of confidence and imposter syndrome, to name but a few. It weighs us down and stops us from living our true and divine purpose. It stops us from believing in the magic of ourselves.

Fear is at the root of such a festering wound. This internalising of the patriarchy has immobilised many wise women and Witches. We hold ourselves back, shame ourselves, ignore our intuition, deny our desires, and belittle our creativity. And when it comes to money, we can be very good at self-sabotaging.

Healing the Wound

The basis of all our personal healing work is connected to some level of trauma from the past, and to trace back further into past lives, whether we remember them or not, is a fascinating subject. Personally, I have no past life memory that

I'm aware of, and yet I do have a deep fascination for certain periods of history and have experienced déjà vu many times.

But if I were to imagine what might have caused my money blocks apart from my own childhood, it's not difficult to see that a vow of poverty on some level in a past life *could* be a contributing factor. Who knows?

Working with this particular part of ourselves is deep work that requires guidance from one who knows and can help us when we are darkened by the shadow of deep trauma. If you feel you need professional help with this, seek it out... there are many holistic practitioners and psychotherapists specialised in the trauma field. Find a good one.

However, there is much you can do magically for yourself if you choose to. You can work with the Dark Goddess, who is an ideal ally for karmic clearing, helping to illuminate our hidden selves, reclaim any lost power and rise up. She brings our shadows to the light. The pathworking with Hekate in Chapter 20 is coming up, but if you feel like doing it now, go ahead. You know yourself best. Let your own magic guide you.

Closing the Gap

When we create distance with our thoughts, feelings and attitudes, we are keeping money out of reach. Often there can be a love-hate relationship with money; we love what it can do for us, but we hate the fact that it's hard to get or keep hold of. It seems that the more we grasp and try to hang on to it the more it escapes us.

How can we close the gap between ourselves and money and make it easier for it to reach us and for us to receive it?

The great thing about being a Witch is that we always have our magical network of support around us in the shape and form of the God/dess force energy to call upon. These spiritual beings are always here and waiting to be asked to step forward and help us with our work when we need them.

Let's think about a being who we can call upon to strengthen our relationship with money and turn it around. Firstly, what destroys that relationship? The ultimate thing that keeps money at a distance from us is fear. Yes, that big ugly ogre who appears on the horizon and strides toward us as he hears our cries of, *I can't afford it... I haven't got enough!*

He feeds on all these cries of unworthiness and grows bigger until all we can see in front of us is this horrible giant who threatens and stops us from seeing our true value. Fear has created a chasm so wide that we are blind to our own magic.

Archangel Michael

There's only one thing that ultimately destroys fear, and that's love. It's true. And the truth, especially in this case, will set you free. It will allow you to move into a space with no restrictions. We are all free spirits, but how often do we allow the chains of fear to imprison us?

I love to work with Archangel Michael and have found that he is a mighty part of the God force for releasing fear and worry. His sword of truth guides us to stand in our own power, and speak our truth, and leads us to inspire others to do the same. He gives us the strength and courage to move out of our comfort zones so that we can be our more authentic selves and step into the magic of our own soul nature. I don't know one person who would not benefit from that kind of presence in their lives, do you?

Some years ago I wrote a song about Michael for a friend of mine who was having a challenging time in her life. I realise now that this song was a prayer, an invocation if you like, but ultimately a tuning into the God force that is Archangel Michael. He has helped myself and a number of other friends who embraced his strength and guardianship at times in our lives when it was most needed.

He's still helping me. For example, the magical being I had in mind for this chapter was not him at all. Michael came into my mind as I was writing, and that, my dear Magical One, is how it happens. This is how we experience the presence of the Gods. We are instruments they will play with, speak to, and communicate with in any way they can through the filter of our thoughts and feelings.

Practise your attunement, keep them in mind and it gets easier, I guarantee it. It's as real as you believe it to be. They will strengthen your resolve and help you to feel worthy of any work you must do in order for your soul to grow.

Witch Ways
Call on Michael

You can ask Michael to help you take away any fear and worries you may have around money and its influence in your life.

Here's how:

- Place some money on your altar and next to it, a representation of angelic energy. An oracle card of Archangel Michael is ideal but not necessary. A white feather, an angel ornament or a piece of angelite or selenite crystal is perfectly fine.

- If you have none of these, improvise with a piece of clear quartz or a hag stone and program it with the energy of Michael by holding it over your heart space and inviting him in.

- Light a dark blue candle or a tea light and make your connection through stillness and silence. If sitting in silence is difficult for you, speak out your invitation in words something like this:

Michael, please come and help me. Take away my fears. I am listening and am grateful for this opportunity to communicate with you, and I am ready and willing to receive your guidance and protection. I know that your love for humanity is one of the greatest forces there is. I am open to receive that love and welcome you now...

Let this be the start of a conversation to be continued in any way that feels right. You may feel that you want to carry on speaking out loud to Michael, speak the words in your mind, or write them down as they flow through your mind. It doesn't really matter. What's important is that you communicate with this spiritual being of light and truth in a way that resonates and works for you.

IN A NUTSHELL

Any past wounds around money can be healed when we understand their origins. In time, as we learn the lessons, we literally give ourselves a spiritual upgrade.

Tuning into the celestial realms will not only raise your energy, but it will bring in the vital healing that you need to move into a receptive state for money to come your way. Yes, you will have to deal with those issues of self-worth, which at first can be overwhelming... but *you're not on your own.* You can slay any dragons with the light of the angelic forces and cast out that nasty little demonic ogre for good. He's a lot smaller than you think.

Now that you're feeling better about money, you're ready for the next step of drawing money to you.

Can you feel it coming?

17
WITCH AT WORK

If you feel safe in the area you're working in, you're not working in the right place – David Bowie

It's time to venture further out of your comfort zone. So you want to turn your witchery into a profession? What a great idea. The world needs more Witches who are richly rewarded for their efforts and skills! Personally, I've found this is something that has evolved slowly over the years. I have embraced every opportunity along the magical path and within my professional practice, to nurture my intentions, develop my skills and grow a life of abundance.

There is a wide range of options available to you to earn a living from your witchery.

Here are just a few:

- Divination - Oracles – Tarot, Runes,
- Seership - Mediumship
- Astrology - Numerology
- Holistic Therapist - Reiki, Rahanni, Reflexology,

Counselling, Sound Healing, Breathwork, Crystal Healing, Colour Therapy, Meditation, Yoga, Massage Therapy,

- Psychotherapy – Hypnotherapy, Life Coaching
- Medical – Midwifery, Nursing
- Animal Husbandry, Animal Rescue, Horticulture, Conservation
- Naturopathy – Herbalist, Homeopath, Ayurveda, Acupuncture
- Artist – Painter, Writer, Tattooist
- Artisan – Craftsperson
- Bard – Musician, Storyteller, Poet
- Priest, Priestessing, Celebrancy
- Shamanic Healer, Practitioner
- Teaching (any of the above)

Whatever your chosen field, you have probably, like I have, been working toward it for some time. Years in fact. You have discovered your natural gifts, you have worked hard, done the training and developed those skills. You are working with at least some or all aspects of the Craft (moon cycles, wheel of the year, ritual, spellwork) in your vocation.
You are confident in your own abilities.
So what's the next step?

Drawing Money to You

By now, you know that abundance is something that is, in fact, an outlook on life. There's more than enough of it everywhere and there's more than enough *in you*. It's right there on the inside and connects you to vast amounts of the same energy outside of yourself.

Let's think of this energy in terms of money. There's plenty of it circulating all around the planet, and it's there to be accessed by you... but there are a number of steps that will help to make it easier to access. And for this part of the journey, we're going to work with some of the magical beings from *The Magic of Nature Oracle* and dive deep into the idea of financial freedom and what it can do for you.

FINANCIAL FREEDOM
Break Away from the Herd – Horse

Becoming willing to move in the direction of money is fundamental in drawing it to you. Now that you have worked on healing those old money wounds, you have freed yourself up to move toward it. Life is an adventure, remember, and this business venture of yours is an extension of that.

With a willingness to learn as much as you can and trust in the process of discovery, you set yourself up for success, because when faced with the inevitable doubts and uncertainty that affect us all, you will take the action needed.

The true authentic power of the will wakes you up in any area where you are asleep. It's that call to action which says *yes* to fulfilling your true creative potential. When I think back to when I first became aware of my magical nature and what it could do for me, *that* was what I wanted more than anything – to realise my true potential and to help others do the same. It's the best intention I've ever had.

In the area of money, are you willing to charge what you are worth and market yourself accordingly? Are you willing to take the risks to discover all there is to learn? Maybe it's a course on starting your own business, collaborating with a partner, or renting a space to work from. If you are willing to do whatever you need to move in the direction of financial independence, it will move toward you.

It's all about energy, and money is a symbol of energy. The problem with money is that we give it so much power and allow it to dominate our lives. By taking our power back and working on ourselves we regain the balance lost and find our financial feet again.

How willing you are to say yes to the freedom that money can give you, transforms your relationship with it.

MAGICAL MANTRA – *Adventure is calling!*

Stay on Course – Swallow

You have all that you need to draw the energy of money to you. You have built up all that inner strength by believing in your own ability. You have planted the seeds of your desire for financial freedom and they are growing because you are paying them attention (what you focus on will expand). You are nurturing and tending your money garden... it really *does* grow on trees, you know!

How do you make your end goal a reality and become a professional in your particular field of witchery?

With the power and focus of a magician, of course. You already have what you need for this, and that is your intention.

By focusing on your intention to be a successful professional, you give direction and purpose to your goals. The power of focus keeps you moving in the direction of money and all it can bring you.

This is a key point. Think about what money represents to you. Is it freedom of choice and independence? Money will give you both of these things and more. So it's not the money by itself, because that's meaningless, but what it actually means to you. Whatever value you give it, it will give back to you. *You give it meaning.*

With the power of your intention in action you will transform your relationship with money, and recognise what gets in the way of that. Anything that distracts you from your true creative path is a drain on your energy... don't fall for it. That is the nature of distraction; it's seductive! It will tempt you in its direction to part with time and money – energy – until you're depleted. Focus does not come from working without distractions, but with a *devotion* so intense that distractions fall from our awareness.

Practise discernment; it's a great teacher and will keep you focused on where you're going. Make a simple list of the things that matter to you and the things that don't. We don't notice the things that don't matter when we are fully focused on what does.

Don't compromise yourself. Remember why you're doing this, what it's going to give you and what you can do with your freedom and independence once you have it.

Money is a by-product of your own energy. It is time and effort you are exchanging for its appearance in your life. Give it the respect it deserves by respecting yourself and notice how much nearer it moves toward you. Stay on the course of your true creative path, focus your intention on abundance and get to work.

MAGICAL MANTRA – *I stay on course*

Embrace Your Creativity – Hare

When you are in touch with your own creative spirit, you know therein lies your potential for success and good fortune. Mother Nature who governs the cycles of work and play is abundant on every level, and your growing awareness demonstrates just how unlimited the idea of plenty is in your life. Through the power of your own creative expression, you will become the great force of nature that you always have been and learn to orchestrate your affairs and grow as a professional.

By embracing our originality and tending to our creations, whatever they are, we learn the art of nurturing and how to nourish ourselves and our relationships. Our openness makes us better listeners and enables us to attend to the practical matters of running a business, and through creative planning, prosperity finds its way to us.

Embracing our creativity teaches us the true meaning of abundance – to be happy with what we have, which is everything we need.

MAGICAL MANTRA – *Creativity flows through me*

Set Realistic Goals – Snail

How many times have you set yourself unrealistic goals and become disheartened when you didn't meet them? I've done it many a time, and every time, I've set myself up for a fall with great expectations that have gone far beyond what I have been capable of. It's all very well thinking that we are unlimited in our potential (non-physical energy) but we must remember we have limited amounts of physical energy, time and effort. We are not superhuman, although we'd like to think we are and some of us behave like it (mentioning no names).

Again, burnout blazes into our lives, reminding us that we must balance our human nature with our spiritual nature if we want to stay sane and healthy. We can channel our energy into making our ideas solid and workable, and develop the discipline and foresight to achieve our goals, but we must know our limitations. We must learn from our experiences and use them to build on. We must set ourselves goals that get us to where we are intending to go but in smaller and do-able steps... and we can increase the size of those steps as our discipline and confidence grow.

MAGICAL MANTRA – *My persistence pays off*

Ask Your Magical Self – Owl

Being open to your intuition is the natural outcome of becoming willing, focusing your intention, and setting realistic goals. It's what happens when all your ducks are in a row and the planets are lined up. When you are focused on financial freedom as an underlying intention, you will be moving towards everything that will provide it for you, but not all at once. You can determine the pace of your work with the awareness of your magical nature, and your inner teacher, as a constant guide.

Owl as a spirit guide will help you to tune into your magical self. He's a great support when any aspects of fear arise, which is only natural on any journey into unknown territory. When you consciously begin to raise your money game, your connection to your own inner guidance becomes crucial at every stage.

Working with Owl will help to eliminate any self-doubt and uncertainty before they become blocks on your path. He also reminds you that to strengthen your intuition and psychic ability, you must acknowledge it and give it the respect it deserves.

If you find yourself asking questions like, *How am I going to afford this?* you are sending out signals for help. And by expecting to receive an answer, you are amplifying your receptivity. Know that help is on its way… the Gods have heard you.

Authentic spiritual guidance directs us to *solutions*. Learn to trust and act on your intuition and it will serve you well.

MAGICAL MANTRA – *I trust in my magical self*

Let Go of Outcomes – Heron

With willingness, focused intention, creativity, setting realistic goals, and asking for help, you have created the circumstances for drawing money to you. Now you must stand aside and allow the higher powers to work their magic for you. This is probably the hardest aspect to apply when it comes to any kind of plan... to relinquish control over a situation when you really want it to work!

Releasing personal effort when you've put so much in might not sound easy, but trusting in the power of divine timing and knowing that the wait will be worthwhile is absolutely necessary at this point. Remember that everything in nature happens at the appropriate time, when the conditions are right. Nothing is forced or pushed into being or doing.

This plan is a spell casting. As long as you have applied the guidance of each step in sequence, continue to develop in those areas, and allow things to happen without the need for control, patience is now your friend. Heron as a guide teaches that patience is not so much about waiting and doing nothing but more to do with trusting that the wait will be worthwhile.

Meditation with Heron will be a useful part of your practice at this time. He will help you to see the bigger picture and to trust in the power of the universe to orchestrate an abundant harvest.

Faith is trusting in what we can't see and *knowing* that it's already here in the invisible realms where it was first created.

All becomes visible in divine timing.

MAGICAL MANTRA – *The wait is worthwhile*

Gratitude – Ladybird

The power of gratitude is the doorway to abundance. Financial abundance is no different, and making a daily practice of consciously giving thanks for everything in your bank account, no matter how much you think you have *or* how little, is an important thing to do. Appreciation is the fuel of gratitude and naturally draws energy of the same vibrational frequency toward you. Your thoughts are a magnet. Choose them wisely.

Ladybird as a spirit guide teaches the power of blessings through the energy of gratitude. Being grateful for whatever life throws at you will keep you in the flow of blessings and allow you to receive the gifts of life. Recognising that everything is a gift, even scarcity, opens you to the lessons of each situation, condition and circumstance.

If we have never known scarcity, how can we appreciate abundance?

In practising gratitude for every lesson that comes our way, we receive its gift and remain in the flow of blessings... the magic of life.

MAGICAL MANTRA – *I am grateful for all my abundance*

Beliefs About Money – Squirrel

Take nothing for granted, be thankful for all that you have and money will continue to find its way towards you. It may come at first in ways you hadn't thought of. Pick up that spare coin, be resourceful, and learn to manage your money better.

Remember that your financial situation is simply a reflection of your beliefs about money and yourself. Here's where Squirrel guidance is helpful because it teaches us that thought alone will not materialise a pot of gold. It's never too late to take stock of your finances and manage your money more efficiently in order to maximise your choices about what you can afford to do. This is the practice of financial freedom, a natural urge to have more so that you can do more and be in a position to help others more.

MAGICAL MANTRA – *I think, act and grow rich*

WITCH WAYS
Money Mantras

A mantra is a specific intention distilled into a short phrase to repeatedly think, say or sing. Using this powerful tool works on the mind and body to influence your actions in every positive way. Money mantras are a fun and easy way to create your magic and cast it out into the universe.

The key factor with a mantra is the feeling behind it. This is easy to do when you're singing and embodying the magic. All the while you're doing this, you are building good relations with the money in your life.

Here are some mantras to open you up to receive money from all sources.

- *Money is my friend*
- *Money grows on the tree of my life*
- *My money mindset is the root of all my financial good*
- *I am worthy of being wealthy*
- *Money comes to me easily and consistently*
- *Money supports me in every way*
- *I am a magnet for money*

A Money Party!

Get a group of friends together who are on this journey of riches with you.

- Time it magically with the new moon or full moon.
- Set your intentions and create a ceremony based on the money mantras above or create your own.
- Sing, drum and dance to raise the abundance vibration.

- Call in the Gods of wealth and riches: Lakshmi, Jupiter, Cernunnos and Oshun.

- Honour the Gods and what they stand for with offerings of stories, songs, mantras and dancing.

- Show your gratitude for the Gods and each other by giving a blessing of wealth and riches: Each person says or sings what they require and desire, and everyone blesses them individually with words of money wisdom.

- Celebrate your new-found riches with music, merrymaking and magic!

- Make it a monthly celebration to remind yourselves how wealthy you are.

In a Nutshell

With the willingness to learn about financial gain, intending it to happen, creating the right environment, and expecting it to come your way, you will have everything you need to convert your money-making ideas into physical currency.

You can also help to turn your witchery into a profession by using mantras as an ally for your work with abundance. It will ground your intentions into the body, reprogram your mind and boost your magic *on every level.*

What are you waiting for?

18
MAGICAL MARKETING

People don't know what they want until you show it to them – Amanda Frances

Magical marketing is the Witch's way of putting out into the world what they create. And given that we work with the magical arts, it makes sense to use the tools we have at our disposal to help achieve the all-important task of visibility and discoverability.

Without becoming known, you and those services and creations that you pour your heart and soul into will not sell. Yes, I said *sell*. Get used to it. Because without selling your creations – which become products as soon as they're finished and have a price on them – they will not survive in the marketplace. And neither will you, because nobody will know about you or your work.

Unless you tell them.

Healthy Mindset

Firstly, you need to check your mindset around marketing and what it means to you. How do you feel about putting yourself and your creations out in the marketplace? Does it excite or repel you? The way you view marketing makes all the difference in how you go about it and what you experience.

See it as a way of helping others, and not about being false or overbearing with hard sell tactics. See it as a multitude of opportunities to share what you do and to inspire people to experience magic in their lives. A way to offer something genuinely valuable to people who are likely to be interested in buying it.

Marketing is the impression we give when we step out and show our work and creations to the world. It's about sharing what we do, making new friends, etc. while being aware that the way we present ourselves can create (or negate) future opportunities to share our valuable offerings with those who might enjoy them.

Your marketing will include online work and in-person events; get used to both and enjoy the process. Remind yourself that ethical marketing can be fun, full of learning opportunities that can open up doors for you and the art-form you love.

Try this practice to clarify what marketing means to you:

Make a list of negative ideas about marketing. After each statement, write a counter-statement looking at the same thing from a positive perspective. For example:

- *Marketing is about faking who you are so that people will like you.*

- *Marketing is about presenting yourself in the best possible way so that people will see what you have to offer them.*

Write down some instances where marketing has positively impacted your life, such as coming across an advert or something similar, for a book, a course, a podcast or an item that you value.

Out of Your Comfort Zone

If you're used to cosying up under the radar and being invisible – something many creatives and Witches love to do – it's time to come out and show yourself. You want to create more magic? Get used to being uncomfortable and commit to the work. And it's not enough to believe in your ability and your creations. You will also need others to share those beliefs and tell their friends.

You need to research your market, understand your audience and position yourself to be seen in the marketplace, wherever that is. Become *findable*.

One of my students is an Avon lady and has been selling her wares in her local area and with a weekly market stall for a long time. Recently she has started selling crystals, and her stall and client base provides a ready-made platform. But although she is working hard to promote her crystals by having a monthly open house in her home, she knows she will also have to transition to an online space to maximise her selling opportunities. Because let's face it, most people are on social media nowadays, and if they know you are too... they can find you and keep up with what you're doing. It's a powerful tool, and you're doing yourself a disservice if you don't use it.

Weaving the Web

Nowadays, having some kind of online presence has become a necessity. Not because it's the only way of being discoverable, but because it's an incredibly powerful assistant for increasing the chances of your work becoming known. Creating a platform has never been easier. You can bootstrap your way with little or no budget to begin with and set up a website for free or at least create a social media page for your work. However, if you have a website, this is your very own digital territory that will enable you to grow an email list you can directly promote to without relying on social media, which is effectively someone else's space.

Something else to consider is what kind of traffic you'll be driving to your website and ultimately what you are selling. Will it be paid traffic whereby you'll be paying for some form of advertising or will it be organic traffic driven by the way in which you promote online? What free content will you create? A newsletter and a blog can help, or any informative videos on YouTube, Instagram or Facebook, plus 'live' streaming. There are many ways of marketing, and the key is finding what works for you.

Time Management

Setting aside time to create and maintain an online presence is crucial. Number one tip: Don't let it interfere with creating your art! That must come first. I'll say that again, *your art comes first.* Your creative time is not flexible. It is *non-negotiable*. You make it a priority and work everything else around it. Goddess knows how difficult that is sometimes, but if you can work with your Warrior energy to focus and tune out distractions, you will thrive in the marketplace.

Discipline plays a major role in being a successful creative no matter what your vocation is.

These are the simple steps to begin building a platform that will help to grow your business. Whether you're selling services, knowledge or products, operating in this space and growing your network is an important part of the professional Witch's job.

On the Ground

It's wise to physically do what you can in your local area. Getting your creations into spiritual and witchy shops will help to promote and sell them, as well as attending spiritual and pagan trading events where you can promote your wares and services to a like-minded audience. Traditional forms of media include press releases in local papers, radio interviews or you could do a presentation or exhibit your work in a public venue.

What I Do

When my sister Tania and I launched *The Magic of Nature Oracle* at a local spiritual gift shop, we held a party there and gave readings and workshops with the cards before and after. I put on a Morrigans Path gig at an old country pub to celebrate my debut novel, *The Madness and the Magic*, and it was a great night. I also did a book signing with brandy and tarot cards in my local village shop for that first book. Start on your doorstep.

When *The Witch Wavelength* came out, I did a book launch at my local yoga studio's Tea and Tarot cafe one evening. I gave a talk, sold and signed books, and the book and my oracle cards have been on sale in the shop ever since. Tania and I did a meet and greet at a local Witch shop last year, and I have done several more book signing events at other shops.

I was invited to give a talk at a local pagan moot last year. I displayed my books, oracle decks and Morrigans Path albums on a table and spoke about my writing in all its formats. Ian took his guitar along and we played a couple of songs, which everyone enjoyed, including us. I've been invited to a similar event later this year, plus more gigs with the band where I can promote the books and the cards with workshops.

As a teacher and a performer, this kind of marketing comes easily to me, because I love meeting people and being sociable. The battle I have is between the extrovert and the introvert. I am mastering the art of shapeshifting into a hermit and hiding away to write, which is an essential part of getting books written. Remember, your creations must come first.

It's Not All Writing

For the past twenty years, I have given readings and healing from my home, which I still do. I have also run tarot and magical courses and workshops from home and in other venues. I recently ran a six-month in-person course based on *The Witch Wavelength* book which I thoroughly enjoyed and so did my students. The hall was next door to a magical wood, so Witch Walking was a regular part of our agenda each month.

Over the years I have also attended many trading events where I've given readings inside and outside, sometimes in busy pubs and shops. This includes a lot of the festivals Morrigans Path have played at and still do.

In March 2022, I started *The Witch Wavelength Podcast* with my husband, Ian, to promote my writing in all its formats and to network with others. I love doing the podcast, as it's something Ian and I can do together, and as we already have the studio gear needed for recording, it's not been an expensive thing to do. We publish twice a month, with guests coming on once a month.

As far as marketing goes, it's a slow burn, but it's a great way of meeting other kindred spirits. I've been interviewed on other witchy podcasts and invited the hosts to come on mine. Plus we get to play our music, and if we have magical musicians on, we play theirs too!

Online

I started off in 2012 with a free website and created pages for my readings, reiki work, workshops, courses and Morrigans Path. Not being tech-savvy at all, I struggled and swore a lot as I learned the ropes. It was painful and took many moons to get my head around any of it.

At the same time I set up relevant Facebook pages and over time have added Instagram and YouTube into the mix. It's all been a learning curve and continues to be. The rate at which technology progresses takes us into constant and sometimes turbulent waters.

We have to ride the waves to a certain extent, but I have discovered (the hard way) to only learn what I need to know when I need to know it. I suggest you do the same. It's easy to become overwhelmed with so much information all at our fingertips. Pick one or two social media platforms to use, and concentrate on those.

I try to keep my online and social media time scheduled if I can, after my writing is done for the day. But sometimes I fall off the wagon and it slips in of its own accord when I've convinced myself I *have* to post, message, or send an email.

If this is you, don't beat yourself up. Get back in the saddle when you can and re-focus. Remember why you're doing it. You're creating magic to share with others. It doesn't get any better than that.

On With the Quest

Needless to say, marketing is an ongoing work in progress, and you will create your own strategies and plans. Having a marketing background is not essential. You just have to be willing to learn and put the time in. Consistently.

For an author, it's said that the best way to market is to write the next book, and while I think that's true, keeping a foot in two worlds is most definitely a requirement. Learning to straddle between the outside world and the pages of my books is a continual balancing act.

I have to sit down and write every day. I do it because I know that practising will make me a better writer. I want to improve and create better books so that they will help and inspire more people. The creative process is my primary focus. If you are a Witch who writes, you know this. If you are a Witch who paints, you know this. If you are a Witch who makes anything and wants to share your creations, you know this. We are in for the long haul... there's no need to rush and there's plenty of time.

Weave this mantra into your daily life:
I market my magic to help and to sell

In one of the podcast episodes, I talked to the lovely Amber, a crystal Witch, who started out doing 'live' sales on Instagram with a budget of a tenner. She did it consistently four to five times a week, and within a year had built up 4000 followers. The money she now earns pays her rent. Clarity of purpose and grit-like determination are key openers of the door to success. You can listen to the audio version of her story here:
bit.ly/44kgAPR

Remember as a Witch, if you are in tune with who you really are, you do not just believe in magic, you live it and breathe it, working it into every day, weaving each thread with the intention of creating exactly what you want.

From this perspective, your marketing is no different. It begins with you and the creation of the product itself.

Branding

Don't be fooled by this term and think you need to reinvent yourself or worse still, shoehorn yourself into a box. Categories and niches are simply tools to be used when your creation is *finished*. Getting caught up in them too early on will choke the life out of your creativity.

How do You Define Yourself?

To begin with, genre is enough. For example, Witch Lit is defined as magical writing, which can be anything from ancient to contemporary in fiction (historical, horror, fantasy, magical realism, romance) and encompasses all pagan, druidic and shamanic traditions (old and new) in nonfiction. Plus poetry and song.

Our witchiness already defines us to a certain extent, but what we do under that umbrella is unique and individual. What kind of pictures do you paint? What sorts of gifts do you make? What do you teach? What kinds of oracles do you work with?

Understand your genre and know what the boundaries are. Then push and move beyond them.

Witches are wildly creative. Don't limit yourself.

You are the brand. Not a trendy logo, a flashy bunch of graphics, some idealised, perfected image or what you think you should be displaying to the world. Quit wasting your precious time on worrying about what you can't control, and concentrate on what you can.

Practise. Create. Do the work. Do it better. Be of service.

This doesn't mean you don't have to plan anything. I planned to write my first book two days before I started writing it for NaNoWriMo (an online challenge to write a novel in a month) back in 2012. I had no idea how I was going to do it, only that I would give it all I had. In a way, I'd been preparing for that moment for most of my life; writing from childhood and experiencing as much of life as I could. Decide on what you're going to *start* to create and the plan will evolve as you go.

Be honest. Be authentic. Be accountable.

We are the result of our own creativity; in full flow, in turbulence and stagnation, in beauty and chaos. At the edge of the unknown is where we evolve and *grow*.

WITCH WAYS

Here's a useful magical marketing practice. Take the time to do it and integrate it into your business routine, and in your place of work. I have all kinds of magical objects and tools floating around in my office, just in case I need to include some magic into my work, which is more often than not.

Pentacle Power

The Pentacle is a magical compass and one of the most intuitive and grounding tools in Witchery. By tuning into its power, we can access the power of Earth, Air, Fire, Water, and Spirit to guide us at all times.

Let's take a look at each in relation to marketing:

- **EARTH** – The Physical: Business and Sales. The power of Health and Wealth.

- **Air** – The Mental: Intellect and Communications. The power of Decision and Discipline.

- **FIRE** – The Creative: Inspiration and Vision. The power of Passion, Purpose and Potential.

- **WATER** – The Intuitive: Relationships and Connections. The power of Networking and Flow.

- **SPIRIT** – The Soul: The Guides, the Gods and the Ancestors. The power of Authenticity and Soul Attunement.

The Marketing Mentors

This practice will help you understand the aspects of the business pentacle and can be very useful to work with throughout the entire building of your magical business.

We're continuing here with the idea of a spiritual mastermind group, but this time the focus is on the marketing and promotion of our services and creations, whatever they might be.

A Business Meeting with the Elements

- Prepare yourself in a sacred space with **solitude, stillness,** and **connection.**

- Draw a large five-pointed star.

- Write the word, *Spirit* above the central point at the top, *Air* at the upper left point, *Water* at the upper right, *Fire* at the lower right point, and *Earth* at the lower left.

- Place a picture, an oracle card or an object to represent an ancestor, angelic being or a chosen deity at the Spirit position.

- Place a feather at the Air position, a shell at the Water position, a tea light at the Fire position, and a hag stone or crystal at the Earth position.

- Contemplate the symbolism of Spirit passing through the four elements, directing and binding everything together for manifesting.

- Focus on the pentacle and repeat to yourself: *I am protected and connected.*

- Close your eyes and see and feel the power of Air blowing into the pentacle... see Water flowing around it... Fire lighting up every point and the power of Earth making it solid.

- Hear the voice of the wind and waves lapping; feel the warmth of the sun on your face and the ground underfoot.

- Absorb the energy into your body...feeling it strengthening and revitalising you.

- You are connected to and protected by the power of the pentacle... and ready to meet your mentors.

- Starting with Spirit, focus on your picture or object... and close your eyes. Call in the spirit being and invite them to join you. Make known your intention to commune with them soul to soul.

- Ask them for guidance on being your true, authentic self... ask any questions you like and write down the answers. Listen and stay with them for as long as you need to, and thank them before they leave.

- Next, move on to Air, take the feather... close your eyes again, and call on the power of communication.
  What decision do you need to make for your business to thrive? How does discipline play a part in its creation? Listen... and write down any answers you receive. Thank the magic of Air.

- Next, move on to Fire, light the candle... close your eyes and call on the power of creativity.
  What is your vision for your creations? Where is your passion leading you? Listen... and write down any answers you receive. Thank the magic of Fire.

- Next, move on to Water, pick up the shell... close your eyes and call on the power of your intuition.
  What connections do you need to make to grow your business and develop your creations? Do any people come to mind who can help you? Listen... and write down the answers you receive. Thank the magic of Water.

- Finally, move on to Earth, pick up the stone... close your eyes and call upon the power of wealth.
  What is the one thing you can do to manage your fi-

nances and improve your sales at the moment? Listen... and write down the answer you receive. Thank the magic of Earth.

- Sit quietly and close your eyes once more... see and feel the power of Air blowing into the pentacle... see Water flowing around it... Fire lighting up every point and the power of Earth making it solid.

- You are connected to and protected by the power of the pentacle.

THE MAGIC IS DONE.

You can draw upon this energy at any time. Call a business meeting with the elements whenever you need to. Treat it as you would a physical meeting... make a date and a time, and show up. Make sure you record your findings.

Alternatively, instead of the elements themselves, you could appoint a member from the spirit realms as a representative of each element. Choose carefully, create your sacred space and they will join you in the ultimate place of power: your imagination.

Be specific, be open and be receptive. Make it a regular practice of intention and discipline and in time, changes will happen.

IN A NUTSHELL

Marketing begins with you and your creativity. Get to know your unique process and embrace the freedom to be your magical self.

If you are a Witch who offers a service, products or knowledge and wants to build a successful business, you need a foot in both the earthly and the unearthly worlds. Whatever your business is about, your magical practice remains at the heart of it.

There are no limits to the fun you can have with your business spirit guides. Be creative, act on the guidance, and learn to pivot and grow.

19
ABUNDANCE HEART-SET

A goal is a dream with a deadline – Napoleon Hill

Feeling abundant is the key to creating it in our lives. And the more we tune into the spirit of abundance, the more we will realise it's already present right there on the inside. So in theory, it is not something we need to create at all, because we already have it. But the creative part is the manifesting of that energy as a result of working out our intentions... those physical actions that bring about the dream and the burning desire. We cannot bypass the physical world and conjure up matter. Yet. Give the Gods time.

Where can we feel abundant? Is it something that develops in our minds? Of course, we can't ignore the power of the mind and the part it plays in our journey to riches, and we have to learn how to use it. Mindset is crucial to the achievement of our goals in life. Without a healthy and positive mindset, we remain stuck in our heads.

However, in this chapter, we are going to move from the head into the heart space. This is the place of our dreams and intentions.

Intention or Goal Setting?

The difference between a goal and an intention is where we set those things in ourselves. Goals are set in the mind, and intentions are set in the heart. A goal is something we work towards one step at a time which is focused on the future, while an intention is something we set out to do overall and is focused in the present. Goals are about reaching a destination and doing what's needed to get there, while intention is about the direction we take on the journey, and who we are being on the way.

For example, you might have the intention to feel more balanced and peaceful with a goal of a daily meditational practice.

Your intention creates your focus and purpose while your goal moves you into alignment with it.

In yogic philosophy, an intention is referred to as a *Sankalpa*. *San* is the Sanskrit term for 'connection with the highest truth', and *Kalpa* means 'vow'. Therefore an intention, or Sankalpa, is a vow and commitment we make with ourselves to support our highest truth.

A great yoga practice for intention setting that anyone can do is Yoga Nidra. This is a practice of lying down, guided by the voice of a teacher, starting with a Sankalpa, followed by a rotational method of relaxation for the whole body. Making an intention in this way helps to sow those initial thought seeds into the subconscious while the mind and body are receptive. Also, if you find it difficult to sit for meditation because you experience a lot of tension, this can help to relax you first. There are many Yoga Nidra meditations to be found on YouTube. Take your pick.

WITCH WAYS
Setting the Heart on Abundance

An effective magical practice for this is to set up an altar specifically for opening the heart to abundance. Place objects and images on your altar to symbolise this magical energy and be as creative as you like. Gather around you anything that helps you to attune to the energy... use candles, oracle cards, crystals and any objects, natural or otherwise, to remind you.

What objects and images give you the feeling of abundance and wealth? I like to place money beside a magnet on my abundance altar; pictures of harvest time, cornucopias, the colour gold, and prosperity deities. I love to use cards and oracles and create my own sigils, which are secret, personalised symbols. You may associate a particular plant, colour or set of symbols based on your own life experience around riches. Use them and indulge in the luxury of immersing yourself fully in the energy of abundance.

There are no rules. Tune into what looks and feels right for you. The symbols we associate with our work are personal to us and the more we develop our own set of correspondences, the more meaningful our magic becomes.

As you know, I like to use hag stones for spells but have found it also helps to have crystals on my altar with properties that harmonise specifically with the abundance vibration.

Here are some examples:

Emerald – The Heart Opener

In the writing of this book, I have been naturally attracted to the stones of riches, one of which is a lovely lump of emerald; a stone of the heart with abundance written all over it.

What has the heart got to do with abundance? Only when our heart is open, do we allow the flow of universal blessings to come into our lives. Emerald is known as a stone of prosperity and has been traditionally used to stimulate wealth by removing thoughts and feelings of unworthiness that block the flow of abundance.

Open-heartedness allows us to receive the gifts of abundance within all of life's experiences, especially in our relationships. The gift of an open heart enriches our lives on every level, and connects us to love and compassion, the magical vibration of abundance.

Emerald also helps us to tune into the vibrational frequency of gratitude and understand that there is no lack or scarcity with true abundance. It is a powerful tool for shifting scarcity consciousness to prosperity consciousness by developing trust in the Spirit of Unconditional Love (our soul), to provide us with all that we need.

Citrine – The Manifestor

For its manifesting properties alone, citrine is a great contender in the financial stakes. Its vibrational charge stimulates our second and third chakras, initiating our creative energy and the will. This empowers our ability to bring energy into form, where manifesting money becomes a joy and a pleasure. It's a stone of optimism, and consequently gives you the courage to try out new things, like a new business venture or a money-making idea.

Garnet – The Attractors and Motivators

TSAVORITE is a green garnet representing wealth in all its positive aspects: financial, creative, emotional, physical, *and* artistic. It helps to cleanse and open the heart like emerald, but also enhances vitality and a zest for living; properties that help to align with our intentions and dreams.

As a carrier of the Green Ray energy, it's an excellent tool for those who have money issues, helping to heal limitations on a physical level. This regenerative aspect of the stone makes them especially useful for increasing productivity, career advancement, and material success.

SPESSARTINE garnets are powerful stones of attraction. They act as a magnet to draw whatever you need to you, be that a job, a lover, a creative project, or anything else that involves personal attraction as a key factor. However, it's a potent stone and must be used with care.

Why? Because it increases the speed at which your intention comes into physical form. Its magnifying qualities of creativity and sexuality make it extremely potent – so be very careful what you wish for. Make sure to tailor-make your magical work so that everything aligns with your intention and pay extra attention to the detail of your correspondences.

For example, it's dark moon as I write this, and I'm taking my time to think about my intentions for the new moon coming up. Spessartine sits on the altar with a very specific intention for the moment, and I trust that it will do its job.

Sunstone – Service to Others

This is a stone of personal power and leadership. It can assist one in the manifestation of prosperity as well as the attainment of knowledge and wisdom. Its properties of solar energy help to connect with higher frequencies of light.

Sunstone is a great transmitter and receiver of blessings, and when worn as a pendant over the heart, can bring the heart's wisdom into alignment with the mind's aspirations. It teaches the power of true leadership as an act of being in service to others, and because of its ability to reveal ego-based desires and motivations, is an excellent ally to work with in business dealings.

Take some time now to reflect on your own feelings and experiences with stones and crystals. Are there any in particular that make you automatically think of prosperity or give you a sense or feeling of abundance? Seek out these stones for your altar or wear them as jewellery, and turn yourself into an altar!

As long as the stones remind you of what abundance means to you, that's the key factor. When the tool resonates with your intentions it will encourage you to work for your goals.

Abundance Incense

To accompany the riches on your altar and raise the vibration higher, what better than some incense made for the job?

Here's what you need:

Mixture

- Cauldron or heat-resistant container
- Mortar and pestle or small non-metallic bowl for mixing
- Charcoal disc for burning
- Dragon's blood – Potency
- Rose petals (dried) – Love and healing
- Cardamom seeds – Love
- Juniper berries – Protection and psychic power
- Patchouli – Fertility and money

- Oak moss – Strength and wealth

METHOD
- Gather the ingredients while thinking about your intention.
- Add each ingredient into the bowl, breaking it down and visualising what it's bringing to your work. What does your intention look and feel like?

Remember that this is a suggestion; there is nothing set in stone here. You can easily choose incense based on what feels right for you. Witchery is a craft and a practice that we engage in with our physical senses as well as our psychic senses.

And if we are to work magic well, we are constantly fine-tuning the integration of both.

The Spell

You can add a hag stone (Earth) to fully ground the higher vibrational energy of the crystals. I like to add a feather (Air) for clarity of mind and place it in the hag stone. A large oyster shell (Water) for emotional clarity contains the dried incense next to my cauldron and a green candle (Fire) for abundance in any of these areas: health, relationships, creativity, knowledge, business and money. You can focus on one or any number at a time.

Once you are set up with all of your tools at your altar, light the candle and your charcoal disc, and while you are waiting for it to turn white, take the time to tune in to the magic inside you. Do this however you like. I usually find what works best for me is to sit in silence and focus on my intention. Next, add your incense in small amounts to the burning (white) charcoal and see your intention flowing out into the universe.

Sing one of your own, or listen to the audio version of the Abundance Chant here: **bit.ly/3XE0VJ7**

I am abundance
I am prosperity
The spirit of love and life is within me
I see on every level
I hear in every way
The universe enriches me in all ways

While you do this, you are weaving every element with Spirit, the eternal essence of yourself and the cosmos. You are raising and directing energy. The inner work becomes the outer work as you step into your Witch power, and *become* abundance.

In a Nutshell

Remember that abundance is first and foremost a feeling. It's not something out of reach. It's already inside you in the trillions of cells of your body, in the air you are breathing in every second, in the thousands of times you think and blink every day.

How magical is your human body? You *are* abundance. And that's just the physical side of you... the non-physical you is unlimited and infinite in comparison. You are a magical creation. Abundance flows through your mind and body.

It lives in your prosperous heart.

20
THE BROKEN HEART

Healing occurs within the divine act of loving ourselves – Christine Jette

What do we do to access abundance when our hearts are breaking? Grief and loss are a part of life. Whether we lose a loved one through death, the break-up of a relationship, or experience the loss of a part of ourselves, the mighty power of grief and its effects on our life can be crippling.

So where's the enrichment in heartbreak? What do we do when our cup runs over with the tears of grief and we find ourselves in the depths of emotional pain?

If we can remind ourselves that the true nature of abundance is that we already have *everything we need*... we have to try and believe that. It's difficult, I know, when you are hurting like crazy and can't imagine it ever going away. However, tuning into the wisdom of the heart will bring healing no matter how painful those feelings are. If you can bear the pain and sit with it, and not try to cover it up or deny it in any way... eventually it *will* lessen.

Letting Go

When we recognise the pain in our thought patterns that has lived in the mind for a long time, we can relinquish its power over us. When we understand that we create our own pain, albeit unknowingly, we don't even have to let go of it because the feeling subsides by itself.

The pain *lets go of us* when our thinking no longer feeds it.

This is a simple and yet profound truth, but how many of us can take that kind of responsibility for the emotional pain that we feel at times of great loss in our lives? I can remember at the age of sixteen, the heartbreak of being dumped by my first love. Oh, the misery! I lay on my bed and cried buckets. It was the worst feeling I'd ever had. I spiralled into such a dark place, and not knowing how to get out of it, remained in a catatonic state for what seemed like an eternity.

Recently, our youngest son broke up with his first girlfriend and the grief between them was raw and palpable. I cried for them both. You can only be there for people while they are going through their pain in the hope that in some way it helps. I light candles every day for all those in need of healing and send out love and strength, in the hope that it reaches them.

I think it does.

The Stages of Grief

In her wonderful book, *On Death and Dying,* Elisabeth-Kübler Ross, MD, explores the five stages of grief and describes them as:

- Denial and Isolation
- Anger
- Bargaining
- Depression
- Acceptance

Nowadays, it's understood that most people don't go through the stages in any kind of usual order, but cycle back and forth among them until they've worked through their grief and reached the stage of acceptance.

When we are hurting so badly, we are so consumed by the power of these feelings, they control us. But if for a moment we are able to see that the extent of the pain itself is teaching us something, and ask what that is; we are moving towards some kind of peace. Unlike the mind and its insidious nature at times, the heart never lies.

Releasing the Pain

Don't underestimate the power of a good cry. It's usually what will come out first. Let it. Suppressing it will not do you any good, you know that. Seek out the help of a listening ear. Reach out to friends and family if you can. They will be your first port of call. Being able to get it off your chest and talk out your pain releases the build-up inside.

Feeling angry is another part of the way our emotional pain naturally expresses itself. Scream like a banshee; roar like a lion. As long as you're not hurting yourself or anyone else in the process, let it out.

Here is a practice from *The Witch Wavelength* that's worth repeating...

A Natural Pain Relief

You may be fortunate to live in the country or by the sea (like I do) but it's not a necessity. However, if you are able to, visit a natural body of water and try this:

- Stand barefoot in the running flow of water in a stream or at the shoreline on a beach (I like to find a rivulet in the sand where the water runs into the sea).

- Think about what you want the water to take away. It might be unresolved grief, the pain of losing someone in a breakup or a passing, or it could be an illness of some kind.
- Feel the water cleansing and purifying your mind, body, and soul... washing away all the emotional toxins and upset.
- State your intention to the spirits of Water and ask them to take away your pain and grief. Here's a simple chant:

> Maiden, Mother and Crone
> Under my skin and in my blood
> and bone
> Maiden, Mother and Crone
> I am Goddess earth and stone

> Wax and full and wane
> I am breathing in and out again
> Wax and full and wane
> I am Goddess healing pain

> Seasons come and go
> I am deep inside the ebb and
> flow
> Seasons come and go
> As above and so below

- Repeat the chant for as long as you can. Thank the spirits of Water and cast an offering into the water. It could be a shell or stone you have picked up on your way and held in your hands while chanting.

- If you're unable to visit a natural body of water, take a healing bath or shower with sea salt and cleansing herbs and use the above chant or make up your own.

Obviously, don't attempt this anywhere unsafe where the current is dangerous, or if you are too ill to move, or instead of qualified medical support. But as an aid to the healing process, it's a useful magical practice that will help.

Other things you can do:

Go for a Witch Walk and intentionally strut out the pain with every stride. Dance it out of your system. Go for a run. Write down your feelings; I wrote some very angst-ridden poetry in my teens!

Vocalising and exercising in some form are effective ways of working your emotions out of the body.

The Abundance of the Heart

The natural wisdom of the heart is love; plain and simple. When the heart is open we are subject to both pleasure and pain. Some people put up such walls around themselves because they've been so hurt in the past. But does it help in the future?

We have to remember that if we can be present with our pain by not dwelling on the past and telling the same story to ourselves, it will subside naturally. This is the power of presence and self-love, one of the greatest gifts of emotional and spiritual maturity.

Asking for Help

Of course, we are never alone in our heartbreak, even though it may feel like it at times. In the Spirit realms, the angels, Gods and Goddesses, ascended masters and guides are there for us, but we must call upon them for help when we need it. Ask and it will be given.

The attachments we have to our pain, whatever the cause, are cords of energy that form between people, situations and emotions. Calling upon a magical being to cut these cords is a useful and powerful practice to free ourselves from any emotion that prevents us from receiving the blessings of abundance flowing through us all the time.

When we are liberated from the fear of pain, our hearts can heal.

WITCH WAYS

Think about what deities, angels or spiritual beings you associate with abundance, and whom you would like to call upon for help.

Here is a dark Goddess perfect for the job of cord-cutting.

A Pathworking with Hekate

Listen to the audio version here: **bit.ly/3JznbOf**

Begin your connection to your magical self and the otherworld with **solitude** and **stillness**.

- Use deep, slow breathing to relax… releasing all the tension in your body and calming your mind.

- Imagine putting down roots of golden light into the

earth, traveling deeper into the ground with every breath. Take in the earth's energy, feel it glowing and flowing around your body, its golden light warming and filling every cell... and let it flow out through the soles of your feet like roots spreading back into the earth.

- Give no attention to your thoughts; let them come and go like passing traffic.

- Engage all your senses, and remember that what you see and hear and what you smell and feel will add power to your experience... building the images around you as you go. Feel the energy flow increasing as you open your mind and shift your focus from the outside world to the inner planes and your third eye centre.

Visualise a doorway leading out of the room... and walk through it, closing it behind you.

On the other side it's dark, and as you carefully make your way you realise you're in a cave tunnel lit by torchlight. You're not afraid, and continue to walk along the dimly lit passageway, until you reach a stairwell, roughly carved out of rock.

Further down you go, drawn by the torchlight and the heady and earthy aroma of herbs.

Eventually, you reach the bottom, and there standing in front of you is a striking woman cloaked in a deep red robe with a torch in each hand. The light catches a glint of silver and you notice a large set of keys hanging from a thick chain around her neck. They clink together as she smiles at you and turns to walk away, and without thinking you follow her along the tunnel, deeper into the cave.

Now you're in a dark hollow, and the torchlight brightens, lighting up the woman in front of you. She turns to face you and speaks in soft earthy tones:

'I'm glad you are here, dear Magical One. I see your entanglements, the cords of fear and pain that bind you to the past. I'm here to release you... from all people, situations, and emotions that keep you in the dark.'

As she talks, you become aware of a tightening around your body, and you look down to see thick cords of rope across your heart and wrapped around your torso.

You can hardly breathe and call out to the woman, 'Please, help me!'

From the inner folds of her robe, she takes out a shiny object and holds it across her chest. You make out the glint of a dagger's blade as it flashes in the torchlight.

The cords are getting tighter and you stumble and fall, collapsing on the cold, rock floor. You can hear the woman's voice as she steps closer to you:

'Breathe easy, Magical One. See how much damage these cords are doing? I will free you from their hold over you... are you willing to surrender?'

Your vision is blurred, and you can't speak, but you manage to nod. You feel the cords loosen as the dagger slices through them.

The woman speaks again:

'Let's bless the past for all its lessons and gifts and release your stories of yesterday.'

As each cord is cut, you hear her call out the name of the person or relationship, and the situation and emotion attached to it; louder at first... and fading into the distance. Each cord for every heartbreak you ever experienced, all the pain you ever felt, the wounds that didn't heal.

You look down at the cords as they fall away. You breathe easily again, moving and stretching your body, and let out a huge sigh of relief.

And when you have your breath back, you turn to the woman and ask, 'Who are you?'

She smiles, before placing the dagger back under the folds of her robe, and holding up her torch once more so that you can see her face. It's a beautiful face with the darkest of eyes and coal-black hair. Her deep red lips curl up at the corners, and she throws back her waves of long black hair and looks straight into the window of your soul.

'I have been here before time itself. I am Hekate, Queen of the Witches to you, dear Magical One; here to guide you through the dark territories of unresolved grief and loss. Here to free you from the sorrow and heartache of the past, in this life and others. I trust you're feeling lighter?'

'I am,' you reply, looking down at the severed cords, 'Thank you'.

She takes your arm and gently guides you to sit down. 'You look tired, come, rest awhile...'

PAUSE FOR A FEW MINUTES

Gradually, you wake from your slumber, glad to see Hekcate is still there with you.

She smiles, raising her torch to your face. 'All is well with you, now. Allow me to lead you back from the edge, and show you the way out... I'm sure you wish to return home. But first, take this...'

She hands you a key.

'What's it for?' you ask.

'It is the key to your own abundance. The love that flows within you. It carries the power of the highest frequency, and will open the door to the realms of knowledge, wisdom, and wealth. It will protect and enrich your life in every way... you'll see!'

Lighting the way she walks slowly back out of the cave and along the dark tunnel and through the dim corridors until you are standing in front of the same door once again. But looking around, you can't see the beautiful woman anywhere. Hekate has gone.

You open your hand and close your fingers over the key. Pushing the door open, you walk through it, closing it behind you.

You are back in the room.

- Breathe in deeply and draw up the earth's energy, and breathe out the memory of your experience.

- Refreshed and fully awake, you are becoming aware of your physical body. Refreshed and fully awake now…you are becoming aware of your physical body.

- Wriggling your fingers and toes, stretch gently if you need to, and when you're ready… open your eyes.

You are fully grounded and free to heal again.
Welcome back.
The magic is done.

Abundance Spell for Healing Heartbreak

Here's something you can do to support the pathworking with Hekate and heal the heart.

You can do it whenever you want to, but the dark moon is the best magical tide for this kind of witchery.

You will need:

Your altar
A pink and a green candle
Temperance tarot card or an oracle healing card
A piece of rose quartz
Healing oil – 3 drops each of tea tree, eucalyptus and lavender oil. Nine drops in total.
Oil burner – tea light – left-over candle wax
A box of tissues

What to do:

- Light the tealight and make up your healing oil. If you

want to create more, you can make up a 10ml bottle of the healing mixture with three equal parts of each oil.

- Add the left-over candle wax to the oil burner and wait until it has melted.
- Add nine drops of the combined essential oils to the melted wax... and inhale that divine healing aroma!
- Place Temperance from the tarot, or an oracle healing card, in the centre of your sacred space.
- Place your oil burner behind the card.
- Set your candles on either side of the oil burner.
- Place the rose quartz in front of Temperance.
- Write on a piece of paper:

> *Take away all loss and grief*
> *Bring my heart peace and relief*
> *Herbs to bring the highest healing*
> *Stone to bring a kinder feeling*
> *Calmer thoughts in me are growing*
> *Seeds of love that I am sowing*
> *By the power of the moon and sun*
> *Blessed be and harm to none!*

- Light the green and pink candle, and hold the rose quartz while reciting the spell.
- Sit with the stone and hold it over your heart, absorbing the energy of love and tranquility.
- Cry if you feel the need.

The magic is done.

In a Nutshell

You have everything you need to keep you in the flow of blessings in your life. The heart breaks open in many ways, through pain and suffering *and* joy and pleasure.

Every experience teaches us something, and while we don't love without hurting... the magic of abundance knows that our heart can hold it all.

21
IN SERVICE

Discover your divinity, find your unique talent, serve humanity with it, and you can generate all the wealth you want – Deepak Chopra

Ultimately, as Witches and walkers between the worlds of spirit and form, we are in service to humanity and Mother Earth. We embody her gifts of magic and healing, by working and using skills that are instinctual or learned through others. The greatest teacher of all is the Great Mother herself and we embody her gifts through our own magical nature, our own divinity.

Deepak Chopra, in his book, *The Seven Spiritual Laws of Success* answers the question of how we are best suited to serve humanity:

> – *When your creative expressions match the needs of your fellow humans, then wealth will spontaneously flow from the unmanifest into the manifest, from the world of spirit to the world of form.* –

These words stare at me from a postcard on the wall next to my desk as I write. They are words of encouragement and inspiration. They nourish my soul and serve as a constant reminder of why I do what I do. How I serve humanity.

Spiritual Community Service

During an interview with fellow author, Lisa Mc Sherry, on *The Witch Wavelength Podcast* – listen to the audio version here: **bit.ly/3CII45Z** – I asked Lisa to describe her priestess role in her life. She talked about her teaching and service in the pagan community. Up until our conversation, I had felt that I wasn't doing *enough* community work and should be doing more. Perhaps chaining myself to buildings and actively doing something other than what I was doing already. But I was forgetting something...

I have been working as a Witch in my community for years. I offer my services as a spiritual advisor, healer and teacher. We live in a small village with its Women's Institute, parish council and church committee; the quirky, conventional stuff of village life. I've always felt a bit of an outsider as the *unconventional* woman who reads tarot cards, does that healing thing called reiki, and works magic in a treehouse, aka the Village Witch.

However, it's all part of serving the community but in a spiritual way. I see my writing, performing and teaching as part of that service too. I was grateful for having that conversation with Lisa, as it was a timely reminder that I *am* doing enough. I just needed to shift my perception and the self-worth issue disappeared.

General Community Service

In the case of more general service in the community, this is how we can help:

- Donating – time, money, blood, food, services, products

- Volunteering and charity work
- Attending community meetings / sitting on boards
- Shopping locally / recycling
- Conservation work
- Adopting / fostering
- Participating in online community forums

Have you done any of this kind of thing before? And if so, how do you feel about it? Would you do it again or would you prefer a different way to give back to your local community?

Find out what kinds of opportunities are available in your area and give whatever you're able to if you can.

Whether you are helping through volunteering or charitable work in the pagan or the wider community, it all makes a difference. You're in service.

Working as a professional is another expression of this. It's another way of serving the community.

There are three core traits we need to nurture if we intend to be successful in our magical profession:

A Desire to be of Service

A desire to be of service brings a magical quality to our work; a healing element that comes from a love for humanity and an enthusiasm to share that love. When we are passionate about and love what we do, we draw to us the loving support of the Gods and the Universe in all our work.

In my spiritual reading and healing work, it very often doesn't feel like work because I love what I do. I used to feel awkward about asking to be paid for a service that felt like just having a friendly chat with someone. But I have realised over the years that the art of listening, advising and holding space for people when they are feeling at their most vulnerable are skills I have learned through my own training and life experience. It is that experience and my time that someone is paying for and I am comfortable with that now because I have learned to value myself.

Belief in the Self

Belief in ourselves is an integral part of being a successful professional. We generate our own energy and enthusiasm out of our passion for what we believe in. I believe in the power of natural wisdom that is innate in everyone. It's the magic of our own divinity that ultimately empowers and heals. It can transform our lives and the lives of others. But I would never have developed that belief had I not strengthened and worked on my own in the first place and known that it's a truth as real as the air we breathe and the earth we walk upon. It's a living thing.

I love sharing the belief in the magic of our own divinity with others because I know how transformational it can be and how it can turn someone's life around. The power of what self-belief will do for you is unlimited when you apply it to any area of your life. As a professional in whatever area of witchery you choose, it will work magic for you, guaranteed.

The professional Witch is businesslike and has great reserves of energy because they trust in their intuition, and follow it. They honour the guidance of their magical nature because they believe it is who they are. They have *become* the intentions and the magic they work and live by.

Willingness to Work

Are you willing to roll your sleeves up and work to make your dreams happen? It could be an initial decision to start charging for what you do, and that can feel like a big step. Are you willing to identify and eliminate everything that stands in your way of a successful business?

Are you ready to make the time and find the discipline to be organised? This is something creatives don't always find easy but order is needed if you want to establish and grow a business. You will need to know what your priorities are, and what jobs and projects you need to focus on so that there is consistent progress toward expansion and growth.

Remember you have the power to create whatever you want but you must be willing to do what needs to be done, and completing projects is an important priority. If you are used to chaos and clutter, ask yourself, *How much unfinished business is amongst this lot?* Time and space are important currencies, and you can't afford to waste either of them!

If you are willing to work, you will have to be practical and balance your time and energy. You need to be in tune with your body and pay attention to what it's telling you; a healthy diet and the right amount of sleep and exercise are vital if you want to be a successful professional. When you take care of yourself by resting when you need to, you replenish your reserves and make room for new and creative energy to flow.

Burnout is not an option, although a regular visitor with many creatives. It usually occurs because the urge to create is so strong, and once in the flow it's hard to stop. I have a Witch friend who's an artist and craftsperson, and always working on a number of projects at the same time. She finishes them eventually, but exhausts herself in the process because her mind is in a constant state of stimulation. I too, have to continually remind myself of the danger of burnout when I smell it in the air.

When you are willing to work, it starts with you and your own energy. How much do you feel you are worth? Valuing who you are is your starting point and determines everything you do personally and professionally.

WITCH WAYS

To make yourself aware of the principles of personal protection and guardianship while you are in service, it's useful to have a magical reminder for the job.

Cord Spell for Protection

This simple cord spell ties in the spiritual guardians for protection to stand at the door of your mind at all times. All that's required is a good length (roughly 60cm/24 inches) of strong cotton. I like to personalise each knot by naming it, as it helps to bond with the energy.

- **Guardian of Peace** – First knot.
  He stands at the outer gate and asks all who would enter if they come in peace. If not, he turns them away.

- **Guardian of Faith and Purpose** – Second knot.
  He admits only influences that keep your mind alert with the belief in your higher purpose in life.

- **Guardian of Love** – Third knot.
  He allows only influences that bring love and keep it alive in your heart.

- **Guardian of Physical Health** – Fourth knot.
  He admits only the states of mind which keep your body working at optimum levels.

- **Guardian of Financial Security** – Fifth knot.
  He only allows the thoughts which bring you financial benefit.

- **Guardian of Wisdom** – Sixth knot.
  His job is to pass on the knowledge which will benefit you and others.

- **Guardian of Patience** – Seventh knot.
  He repels all impulses to hurry and be impatient with the power of time.

- **Guardian of Strength** – Eighth knot.
  He admits only the influences leading to the growth of courage and confidence.

- **Guardian of Creativity** – Ninth knot.
  He transmutes all negative energy into creative energy and directs it to the service required.

As you tie in each knot, contemplate the spirit of each guardian and what service they are providing for you. The price for their services is your acknowledgment and eternal gratitude. Make sure it is given freely and you will find that these great spiritual forces give you the protection you need at all times.

You can either wear the cord around your neck or your wrist, or carry it with you.

In a Nutshell

With a strong desire to be of service, belief in yourself, and a willingness to work... there is nothing you cannot achieve. You empower and help others by empowering yourself.

Are you feeling generous?

Reaching out in thought, word and deed enables you to spread your magic around and share those gifts... which we move on to next.

22
SHARING YOUR GIFTS

The act of sharing is one of generosity – Austin Kleon

Prosperity, success, good fortune, wealth. *Riches.* Is it possible for an ordinary Witch to have all this going on in their life? Most definitely it is. By now you will know that abundance has been there all the time. You may have had to dig deep to find it, but it's been worth the effort. It has shown up in all kinds of ways because you have believed that it would and had faith in your abilities. Now what will you do with it?

What is the point in practising as a Witch and working magic, if you don't share it with others? Why keep it all to yourself?

In *The Magic Of Nature Oracle*, the words I wrote for the meaning of the Harvest card come to mind:

- *A time of successful completion and flowing abundance which is more than the attainment of possessions and the acquisition of material wealth.*

- *A time of fruition and receiving the benefits of all good efforts.*

- *A time to enjoy some well-deserved success in your life.*

- *A state of consciousness that cannot help but reach out*

beyond itself and enrich all those it touches.

Abundance is all of these things.

Now that you can see how abundance flows through every part of your life, you can't unsee it, can you? Or at least I hope you can't. Abundance is the natural life force running through the rivers and oceans, expanding across the skies, and flowing through the earth's core. It's held in every grain of sand and beams out of a trillion stars. It flows in me and it flows in you.

How can our lives not be magical with abundance around? Tuning in to its high frequency raises our sights, lifts our spirits and opens us up to live magically. We create a magical life when we believe in our own abundance.

We'll only see it when we believe it.

Sharing Our Riches

When we have enriched our minds and hearts with the flow of blessings, it's not something to hold on to. Where is the joy in being fortunate and prosperous if you cannot share your good fortune? So let's turn the abundance chant to *you*, my magical friend...

You are abundance
You are prosperity
The spirit of love and life is within you
You see on every level
You hear in every way
The universe enriches you in all ways!

How Will You Share Your Riches?

I don't think it's something you can work out, or even do. Because your soul had it worked out long ago, and you are already doing it. This is the work of seeking and finding all the barriers within yourself that you have built against your riches. Ultimately, it's not so much about what you do, but more about who you *are* while you're doing it. And while you have worked your magic to become a better this or that, *who you are* is still fundamental to how your life works out for you.

I've said this before, but the power of the word is a mighty force, and combine that with the power of the present moment and you have the power to create whatever you intend. The words *I am* are the God/dess force speaking through you, a spell casting in action. When you say those two words, you become whatever follows them... *I am abundance.*

Giving

Sharing the riches of our souls is about giving, and one of the most valued commodities is our time. I like to share time and space with people. But if I cannot give the time, then I will give other things. I have a friend, Jenna Miller, who I interviewed on *The Witch Wavelength Podcast* – listen to the audio version here: **bit.ly/3XohmZK**.

Jenna runs a local dog rescue charity and does great work. I would love to help out and give a dog in need of a home some love but with three dogs already in our house, it's not a practical option for us. The next best thing is to give money and so I bought a number of printed calendars from the charity as Christmas presents. To have helped in some small way gives me great pleasure.

Do what you can.

A Warm Heart

If you are sharing professionally, you will have done your training and be selling services, knowledge or products. The heart of your work will be focused on the customer's needs. If you work with your creativity from this loving place of connectedness, abundance will flow out of you and show up in many ways. Being generous with your time and energy is an amazing way of doing this.

If you have a genuine love of people, nothing will give you greater pleasure than to share what you have with them. Our time is one of the most valuable things anyone can share with another. Think about your friends and how much time you give them. It's not something we calculate and work out, is it? We freely give of ourselves because we naturally want to share with others.

The Gift of Friendship

I have always valued my friends greatly and loved them. Friendship is a spiritual gift that teaches us so much about ourselves and each other because our hearts are open, our minds are stimulated, and abundance flows in huge quantities between us. We give of our time, our efforts, and our love to another person for no other reason than because we want to.

We learn empathy in abundance through our friendships, as we listen to each other's troubles and provide a shoulder to cry on when needed. We are connected by the divine flow of feelings that help and heal, and through these loving relationships we become flexible and compassionate.

Most Witches are attuned to this healing energy. Our hearts expand, and we are drawn to situations that require our natural empathy and accommodating nature. If this sounds familiar, it's important to remember that with a heart so naturally open, you must guard your energy from others who will drain it off for their own needs.

They may not be aware of what they're doing on a conscious level; you simply have something to give that they need. However, if you are aware of this, see it as an opportunity to adjust the emotional flow in your relationships so that you are not doing all the giving. Friendship is a two-way street. Depletion will leave you running on empty and can lead to resentment and blame, which will only drain you more.

As an open-hearted Witch, you must focus on balance in all your energy exchanges, including friendships, and remember that the power to help and heal flows through you and not *from* you. A good spirit guide for this purpose is the Willow tree. In *The Magic of Nature Oracle* the enchanting energy of Willow connects us to the abundant and divine flow of blessings that help and heal. Attuning to the magic of this tree will guide you to express and share your healing ability.

WITCH WAYS
Pathworking with Willow

Listen to the audio version here: **bit.ly/3NOfhmU**

Begin your connection to your magical self with **solitude** and **stillness.**

- Using the breath to relax your mind and body, inhale positive energy and feel it moving through every layer of your being. As you breathe out watch this positive energy as it becomes a golden glow around you. Feel its warmth and protection holding you, bask in the light as it radiates around you and through you, relaxing every muscle and cell.

- Feel your connection to the earth in every breath you give and take, grounding and flowing in and out of your body.

- Keep breathing deeply and easily, paying no attention to the passing traffic of your thoughts. Your mind is like a millpond, and as your thoughts ripple out it brings a deep sense of calm and stillness. You are totally relaxed and held in the arms of the Great Mother.

- Now you are shifting your focus from the outside world to the inner planes and your third eye centre.

Imagine a doorway, and walk through it, closing it behind you.

You see a path on the other side and begin to walk slowly alongside a farmyard track out and into the countryside. Fields and open land surround you and the air is warm and buzzing with bees and birdsong.

The path leads you to a field where a stream runs through to a wood on the far side. You can hear a skylark singing overhead, and as you look up to spot it, you stumble on some uneven ground and your ankle gives way as you fall.

It's painful, but you hobble along, following the stream as it gurgles and winds its way around clumps of moss and stone.

Your ankle is very painful now, so you're relieved when you catch sight of a huge willow tree on the grassy bank. You need to rest.

Collapsing beside the tree you lean against its trunk, rubbing your ankle which is already swollen.

You notice how the willow stoops over the stream, its leaves combing the water as it trickles along, and you feel comforted by its presence. You feel safe beneath its canopy of branches, bending and flowing with the water, and held by the steadiness of the earth. It's not going anywhere...

'And you don't need to go anywhere, dear soul... and yes, I am Willow, the healer... here to give you strength and to help you see the magic of your own ability. Look how I bend and flow... how I'm part of the water and also Mother Earth. She holds me in her embrace and nurtures my growth. She holds you too. I am stronger because of her, and so are you.

Can you feel the pulse from my heart to yours and back to our mother? It goes around and passes through us, grounding and balancing, and making us whole. We are all as one, connected by our exchange of one to another, yours and mine and the Earth Mother. Our hearts beating together... can you feel it, Magical One?'

It feels like you're in a dream – the tree speaking to you – and yet, it feels quite natural here in this place. But yes, you can hear a steady pulsing like a drumbeat in the distance... and it's getting closer. You can feel the heart of the tree beating through you and merging with yours.

And you can hear the voice of Willow...

'Ah yes, *now* you feel it, don't you? We are one. This is balance, a fair exchange. Back and forth we go. Remember how it feels, Magical One. In *all* your exchanges there is give and take. You can be flexible, you can accommodate another, you can give of yourself... but don't compromise. Do not allow another to take more than you are prepared to give at any one time.

Recognise the imbalance of energy, the tipping point... this is a moment of truth. Withdraw yourself and give *back* to yourself. Time is the great healer. Time to retreat. Time to rest and recover, recharge and rejuvenate.

Listen to your heart, the pulse of the Earth Mother, beating in you and beating in me... can you feel it?'

PAUSE FOR A FEW MINUTES

As you come out of your dream time, all is well. The tree is still supporting you, and you are feeling stronger. The pain from your ankle has subsided and no longer aches. The birds are still singing, the stream gurgling and flowing, and *no one* is talking, not even the tree.

And you can feel the heartbeat of the earth pulsing through you and the tree... and back to the earth... round and around.

Eventually, you get up from your resting place, lean against the tree once more, and say thank you.

Your open heart expands even more... you understand the difference between empathy and compassion. You know what it is to feel the pain of another, and you know the call to act in the service of another and care for their needs. You also know how to honour your own needs and care for you, without compromise.

You trust in the magic of healing and you know how to share it, unconditionally.

You begin to walk back alongside the stream at the edge of the fields, through the open countryside... finding your way back to the path and the farm track. Finally, you reach the end of the path and walk back through the door, closing it behind you.

You're back in the room.

- Breathe in deeply, drawing up the earth's energy, and breathe out the memory of your experience.

- Refreshed and fully awake, you are becoming aware of your physical body. Refreshed and fully awake now, you are becoming aware of your physical body.

- Wriggling your fingers and toes, stretch gently if you need to, and when you are ready... open your eyes.

You are fully grounded, and open to the ways of healing. Welcome back.
THE MAGIC IS DONE.

Return to the healing wisdom of Willow whenever you need to. Do not underestimate the power of its gentle spirit as it shows you the magic of nature and her precious gifts.

IN A NUTSHELL

Gifts are for sharing. Time, money, a personal creation, skills and talents, enthusiasm, a smile, a kind word. Whatever those gifts are – and each one of us is uniquely gifted – will be appreciated by others.

Witches are magical people. Creative people. We work our magic to develop ourselves. To become better human beings. We create our gifts for the world.

23
CELEBRATING THE MAGICAL LIFE

I believe that owning our worthiness is the act of acknowledging that we are sacred – Brenè Brown

It's time for celebration. Your abundance is worth that and more. Now that you have seen it and know it is present in every moment, you will naturally create it in your life. If it's material success you want, you can manifest it. Financial freedom is available to every one of us when we believe it's possible. If you believe it will work out, you will see opportunities. If you believe it won't, you will see obstacles.

If it's the riches of successful and loving relationships, you will attract them. You are perfectly loveable and deserve it. If it's a prosperous and healthy body, you can develop it and enjoy it. Your health is your wealth, remember? If you want a deeper and richer spiritual life, it will reveal itself and unfold before you.

Trust in the magic of your soul.

You have dreamed and visualised, made your intentions and followed through with the right actions. You have performed the ultimate act of magic on yourself and transformed those lower vibrations of self-limiting thoughts to the higher frequencies of unlimited abundance. You have given up your attachments to needing anything because you know you already have everything you need to create your magic.

What Now?

Celebrating who you've become will boost your spirit with one of the highest vibrations there is: **JOY**. And remember, it's all about the feeling. One thing I ask... invite me to the party. I would love nothing more than to celebrate with you. We've come through some interesting times together, and with some magical help from all departments, you've discovered your riches.

The Seer showed you your past, present and future. With the guidance of Amergin you found your focus. The Grail Maiden and the ogre of lack showed you the power of your feelings, the Morrigan gave you strength and courage on the battlefield, while Hekate cut the cords of all those unhealthy attachments. Archangel Michael took away your money worries, while the Gods and the Ancestors brought their insight and stability. The tarot appeared as a visual reminder of your intentions, whereas the crystals grounded and raised your energy, and of course, the moon showed her many faces of yin while the sun beamed out the yang. Willow has shown you how to heal, and throughout all of it, Mother Earth has sustained you and held you in her healing presence.

You have paved your way along the road to riches with every crafting and practice, discovering the life force of abundance in the magic of the seasons, trees and animals. You have walked your spells, chanted in gratitude and danced your praises. You have sat with your prayers and shown your commitment to serve because you know it is in giving that you receive.

But we have only scratched the surface of a vast and infinite source of unlimited power. We have only just begun to see how true prosperity creates experiences that are rich with meaning and purpose. This is the success of co-creation, of manifesting all that you have worked to become... and now, my friend, you can enjoy the fruits of your labours.

Celebration

Celebrate your creations, your passions, your purpose, and know that *they have found you.* Celebrate your witchiness in all its magical forms, and give thanks for the tools of your craft. They are the tools that bring you happiness and health, wisdom and wealth. And the more you practise your craft and tailor-make each tool to work in its own way for you, the more your magic will resonate with others.

Creating a magical life of abundance is a lifelong journey. It will continue to take you into unknown territory, and urge you to move beyond your comfort zone in every area of your life. You will be called to flow with the changes and dive deep into the mystery of your current incarnation and grow.

You will empower yourself. You will transform your life with every celebration. And that's something I am always grateful for in Witchcraft: the fact that there are so many festivals, sabbats, esbats, and joyous times to gather and celebrate together.

The more we see abundance flowing, the more reason we have to celebrate, so that over time, our whole life becomes a magical one. The lines blur, our passions become our purpose, work becomes our vocation, our creativity becomes an expression of our true selves.

Our magical nature reveals our divinity: the sacred and mystical self.

Whether we are celebrating a traditional festival or a personal achievement of some kind, it gives us the opportunity to relax and be carefree, to share in the bounty of our good fortune. I have always loved a party, and can't think of a better reason to have one than celebrating the magical life!

Enriched by the Crone

At the time of writing, I am turning sixty. To mark the occasion, a Croning ceremony with my coven sisters will be on the cards in the near future. Celebrating this rite of passage feels quite momentous, and apart from my human nature kicking in with the fear of facing my own mortality, I know that my magical nature is overriding it. I am grateful for this.

The Crone has been a large part of my life for about fifteen years now, inspiring me in many ways with her wisdom and insight. As a woman and a Witch, my life has been enriched and transformed by her presence and will continue to be. I know this and I'm glad to have her around. She's a great companion and a lifelong friend.

And so the last practice I am offering you is a magical meeting with her. This is very much part of my own practice, and her guidance is always useful and light-hearted. We need humour when we have spent time in earnest on our journey. What better way to celebrate this milestone on our road to riches than with one who is both worldly wise and otherworldly?

Enjoy your time with her.

WITCH WAYS
A Pathworking to Meet the Crone

Listen to the audio version here: **bit.ly/3NsIBxE**

Begin your connection to your magical self with **solitude** and **stillness**.
Using the breath to relax your mind and body, inhale positive energy and feel it moving through every layer of your being. As you breathe out watch this positive energy as it becomes a golden glow around you. Feel its warmth and protection hold-

ing you. Bask in the light as it radiates around and through you.

- Relax and sink down into your body, sending your roots down into the earth, and feel its energy flow through every cell of your being.

- Feel all the tension from your muscles fall away and let go of any thoughts of the outside world, shifting your focus to the inner planes and the third eye centre.

You can see a bright light glowing and it's getting closer...

You move into the light and through it, and on the other side is a path leading to a forest up ahead. You begin to walk along the path strewn with autumn leaves of every colour – deep reds and oranges, golds and yellows – and you breathe in the scent of pine and ferns all around you as you enter the forest.

A crow swoops in front of you, calling out loudly, and lands on a nearby tree... and when you reach the tree, it flies on ahead where it lands again on another tree and waits for you.

You follow the crow through a thicket of ferns and bracken... where it eventually widens into a circle of trees... a grove of silver birches. The crow lands on the branches of one of the trees and flaps its wings, calling out loudly again.

'Oh be quiet, bird... you're always making a damn noise!' cries a gravelly voice, as loud as the crow's.

You turn to see an old woman sitting by a fire in the centre of the grove.

'Well, don't just stand there! Come and join me...' she says, 'I've been expecting you.'

Saying nothing, you make your way over to the fire and sit down next to her on a tree stump rolled over on its side. The old woman rests on a knobbly stick, one hand over the other, and stares into the flames. 'Riches, am I right? Is that what you're looking for?'

'Yes,' you mutter, 'I suppose so.'

She laughs, and the crow starts up again, 'I said quiet, bird!' She swivels round to face you, her bright eyes crinkling at the corners. 'Well, I have a very simple answer to that my dear magical one and it's this: Your task here is not about seeking riches, but only to find the barriers inside yourself that you have built up against them.'

'Is that it?' you say.

She nods her head once and returns her attention to the fire.

'Once you have done that and broken those walls down, you will find that what you are looking for is actually looking for you, do you see?'

You hesitate before nodding slowly.

'Now is there anything else?' she says, 'What guidance do you need? Ask away! Be clear about it... and as long as that bird keeps quiet, I'm all ears.'

Ask the Crone whatever you want and listen...

PAUSE FOR A FEW MINUTES

After the Crone has given you her answer she reaches into the fire and pulls out an object. She cups it in her hand for a moment while it cools and hands it to you. 'Look after this gift...and remember to share it, that's where the magic is. Now be on your way and take that god-forsaken bird with you... go on!'

The crow calls out from the sky, and you follow his cries as he swoops between the trees and back through the forest. You make your way over the bracken and fern and onto the path once again, walking away from the forest and back toward the light glowing in front of you.

You're back in the room.

- Breathe in deeply, drawing up the earth's energy, and breathe out the memory of your experience. You will retain whatever you need to.

- You're feeling refreshed and fully awake, becoming aware of your physical body. Refreshed and wide awake now, you're back in your body... back to yourself.

- Wriggling your fingers and toes, stretch gently if you need to, and when you're ready... open your eyes.

You are fully grounded, and enriched by the wisdom of the Crone.
Welcome back.
THE MAGIC IS DONE.

Remember that you can re-enter the forest at any time and go back to the Crone's silver birch grove. She will be there waiting for you.

How did the Crone answer your question? Remember when travelling in the inner worlds, symbolism is the common language. Write down your findings. If you don't understand the information you receive at first, at least you can refer back if something comes to light at a later date.

What did she give you? Think about its enriching significance in your life and how you can share it with others.

IN A NUTSHELL

Riches for Witches is about transforming the lower frequency vibrations in our energy fields into the higher vibrations of self-wealth and abundance. All the self-limiting ideas and beliefs we hold onto, mostly unknowingly, are made visible and known to us through waking up to our true magical selves.

We do this by applying our magical practices, the medicine that heals the wounds of lack and limitation. We do this through the development of richer thinking, feelings and actions. We do this by listening to and acknowledging the soul's guidance that comes from valuing the self and acting in accordance with our highest and truest aspirations.

This is how we find our gold. I trust that you will find yours. Celebrate the magic of yourself. *Your riches.*

May your soul's journey onward be fruitful and abundant.

Travel well, Magical One, and blessed be.

THANK YOU

I hope you enjoyed reading *Riches for Witches* as much as I did writing it! If you can spare the time for a short review on Amazon, I would be very grateful.

Thank you! Your help in spreading the word is much appreciated.

Audio Links

Type into your browser and enjoy!

Pathworkings

- CH 2 – The Seer – **bit.ly/3ptorLX**
- CH 3 – Grail Maiden – **bit.ly/3NLByBy**
- CH 5 – Your Magical Nature – **bit.ly/44zGLlN**
- CH 6 – Magical Mastermind – **bit.ly/43Uyxo1**
- CH 8 – Amergin – **bit.ly/3piXA5e**
- CH 11 – Winter – **bit.ly/42Yc8oA**
- CH 13 – The Morrigan – **bit.ly/3NqIVwN**
- CH 14 – The Sun – **bit.ly/3plykLK**
- CH 20 – Hekate – **bit.ly/3JznbOf**
- CH 22 – Willow – **bit.ly/3NOfhmU**
- CH 23 – The Crone – **bit.ly/3NsIBxE**

Podcast Episodes

- CH 18 – Amber Rose, Crystal Witch – **bit.ly/44kgAPR**

- CH 21 – Lisa McSherry, Author, Teacher, Priestess – **bit.ly/3CII45Z**

- CH 22 – Jenna Miller, Warrior Witch – **bit.ly/3XohmZK**

Morrigans Path Songs

- CH 2 – Mothers Chant – **bit.ly/43NOrRf**

- CH 4 – Not a Dream – **bit.ly/3Nl4NKd**

- CH 5 – Earth Chant – **bit.ly/3NJhDmW**

- CH 6 – Warrior Queen – **bit.ly/3JwNOn8**

- CH 12 – Morrigans Prayer – **bit.ly/3JtbTuZ**

- CH 9 – Draw her Down – **bit.ly/3Pu9R1n**

Musical Mantras

- Intro/CH 1/19 – Abundance Chant – **bit.ly/3XE0VJ7**

- CH 5 – Wholeness Chant – **bit.ly/3qqVIxm**

FURTHER READING AND RESOURCES

Money & Success

Sacred Success – Barbara Stanny
Rewire For Wealth – Barbara Huson
Overcoming Under Earning – Barbara Stanny
Rich As F**k – Amanda Frances
Quantum Warrior – John Kehoe
Think and Grow Rich – Napoleon Hill
The Science of Success – Wallace D. Wattles
The Trick to Money is Having Some – Stuart Wilde
The Little Money Bible – Stuart Wilde
Money Magic – Jessie Susannah Karnatz
Creating Affluence – Deepak Chopra
Your Invisible Power – Genevieve Behrend

Dark Goddess Spirituality

Celtic Lore and Spellcraft of the Dark Goddess – Stephanie Woodfield
Celtic Women's Spirituality – Edain McCoy
The Guises of the Morrigan – David Rankine & Sorita D' Este
The Book of the Great Queen: The Many Faces of the Morrigan – Morpheus Ravenna
The Morrigan: Meeting the Great Queens – Morgan Daimler

Spells & Rituals

Everyday Sun Magic – Dorothy Morrison
   Sun Magic – Rachel Patterson
   Moon Magic – Rachel Patterson
   Spells for Living Well – Phyliss Curott
   The Book of Ceremony – Sandra Ingerman
   Dark Moon Mysteries – Timothy Roderick

Herbals & Stones

The Book of Stones – Robert Simmons and Naisha Ashian
   The Crystal Bible – Judy Hall
   A Green Witch's Cupboard – Deborah J. Martin
   Encyclopedia of Magical Herbs – Scott Cunningham

Wisdom & Well-being

Anam Cara: Spiritual Wisdom from the Celtic World – John O'Donohue
   Listening to the Oracle: The Ancient Art of Finding Guidance in the Signs and Symbols All Around Us – Diane Skafte
   On Death and Dying – Elisabeth-Kübler Ross
   The Heartmath Solution – Doc Childre and Howard Martin

Marketing

Perennial Seller – Ryan Holiday
   Show Your Work! – Austin Kleon

Tarot & Oracle Cards

Vision Quest Tarot – Gayan S. Winter & Jo Dosé
   The Magic Of Nature Oracle – Sheena Cundy & Tania Copsey

The Wildwood Tarot – Mark Ryan & John Matthews & illustrations by Will Worthington
The Minoan Tarot – Laura Perry

Tarot Books

Seventy-Eight Degrees of Wisdom – Rachel Pollack
Mastering the Tarot – Juliet Sharman-Burke
Tarot for the Healing Heart – Christine Jette
The Magical World of the Tarot – Gareth Knight

Resources

HeartMath® – **bit.ly/3pLd9mI**
Facing North – **bit.ly/3Q3pSeV**
Witch Lit Facebook Group – **bit.ly/44RvHR6**

Acknowledgments

Writing and publishing independently requires the wearing of many hats which can weigh heavy on an author. My gratitude goes out to these professionals for lightening the load:

Laura Perry and Daniel Allison for their guidance and support with the development and editing process.

Fiona Herbert for excellent proofreading skills.

Katherine Genet for an enticing foreword.

Fiona Jayde for the great cover.

My husband, Ian, for recording and producing the audio files.

Tuned in all the way.

Sterling job, everyone!

Also by Sheena Cundy

Non-fiction

The Witch Wavelength: Tuning in to Your Magical Nature
The Magic of Nature Oracle

Fiction

Witch Lit Series
The Madness and the Magic
Bonkers and Broomsticks
Chaos in the Cauldron
Witch Lit Box-set
Witch Lit Audiobook

Music

Morrigans Path

ABOUT THE AUTHOR

Sheena Cundy is a songwriter, podcaster, tarot reader and Reiki master.

She lives in Essex, UK, with her husband, Ian, their sons', Leon and George, and three mad Spaniels.

www.sheenacundy.com
email: **craftycrones.org@gmail.com**

For Witchy tips, book/course updates and offers, sign up to Sheena's Treehouse Magic Newsletter: **bit.ly/3ArmbGm**

Printed in Great Britain
by Amazon